POSSIBLE IMPOSS- IBILITIES

A LOOK AT PARA- PSYCHOLOGY

BY ELIZABETH HALL

HOUGHTON MIFFLIN COMPANY BOSTON 1977

Also by
ELIZABETH HALL

Phoebe Snow
Stand Up, Lucy
Why We Do What We Do
From Pigeons to People

Library of Congress Cataloging in Publication Data

Hall, Elizabeth, 1929–
  Possible impossibilities.

  SUMMARY: Discusses the field of parapsychology
today and the experimentation in it.
  1. Psychical research—Juvenile literature.
[1. Psychical research] I. Title.
BF1031.H219   133.8   76-58529
ISBN 0-395-25299-7

When I used to read fairy tales, I fancied
that kind of thing never happened, and
now here I am in the middle of one!

Lewis Carroll,
Alice in Wonderland

For my grandson,
Scott David Anderson

CONTENTS

PART ONE
Telepathy and Clairvoyance

"I see nobody on the road," said Alice.
"I only wish *I* had such eyes," the King remarked in a fretful tone. "To be able to see Nobody! And at that distance, too! Why it's as much as *I* can do to see real people, by this light."

Lewis Carroll,
Through the Looking-Glass

1

The Red Ace of Spades

Plates fly off shelves, doors slam, and light bulbs shatter whenever a fifteen-year-old girl comes into the room. Spoons melt and bend, and stopped clocks begin to run, when a young man passes his hand over them. A woman has a dream in which her brother dies; the next morning word comes that he died during the night. A camera takes pictures although the lens is covered and the young photographer is across the room. Using an alphabet code, a dog taps out answers to questions. A woman says she can see into the future.

Stories like these appear in the paper nearly every day. Television talk shows bring us psychics, persons who say they can read minds or foretell the future or move objects without touching them.

Most people are familiar with such claims, and many of

us wonder how much we can believe. A few years ago the answer would have been easy: none of it. But things have changed. Parapsychology has become respectable, and more and more researchers are taking some of the claims seriously.

Despite its new respectability, parapsychology is not welcome everywhere. Highly publicized cases still don't stand up to scientific scrutiny. Publicity seekers still pretend to have mysterious powers. After nearly a century of trying, researchers still have not been able to produce solid evidence that people can sense others' thoughts or see into the future or move objects with the power of their minds. But in laboratories in many countries, quiet experiments that don't appear in newspapers are giving us hints that such things as telepathy do exist — even though we can't say just how they work, or why.

People hear about these tantalizing experiments and wonder why psychologists can't go back to their laboratories and settle the question. It seems as if a few careful experiments ought to give us the answers we seek. But it's not that simple. So far, the answers seem to be a combination of yes, no, and maybe.

Before we look at the evidence, we ought to know what we're looking for when we speak of parapsychology. Psychology is the study of human behavior, and *para* here means "beyond." *Parapsychology* is the study of behavior that goes beyond what we believe is possible. Some people call this kind of behavior *psychic* or *psi*, others call it *paranormal*, or beyond the normal. Parapsychology covers many different things, but all parapsychology, at first glance, seems to break the laws of physics.

If the universe runs according to the rules in the textbooks, parapsychology is impossible. People can't read minds. They can't see into the future. They can't hold a missing person's handkerchief and know all about that person and where he or she is at the moment. They can't affect the growth of plants. They can't leave their bodies and flit about the room. They can't remember past lives.

But the rules in the textbooks are changing. Twenty years ago, everyone was sure that people could not control the way their hearts beat, their body temperature, their blood pressure, their brain waves, and all the other bodily systems that seem to work by themselves. Today we know that most people can learn to control at least some of these systems.

Twenty years ago, we saw human beings and the universe through the eyes of Western science. Anything that didn't fit that view of the world, we either pretended not to see or said was just a trick. We all knew that Indian holy men who wrapped white cloths around their middles and lay on beds of nails were tricking us. And we didn't believe them when they slowed their hearts almost to a stop, or were buried for days and then stepped gaily out of their graves. We were too smart to be taken in by cheap stunts.

Smart as we were, we sometimes fooled ourselves. Psychologist Jerome Bruner once showed people photographs of playing cards and asked them to tell him what they saw. One at a time, these people came into a room, sat in a chair, and watched playing cards appear on a screen before them. Without hesitation they called out each card and its color as it flashed on the screen. But Bruner had rigged the deck. His ace of spades was red, not black. Few people noticed anything odd about the card. Some said they saw a black ace of spades. Others were sure it was a red ace of hearts. Twenty years of seeing black spades and red hearts had so influenced their expectations that their brains failed to report what their eyes saw.

People in different countries expect to see different things. Thirty years ago, Mexicans didn't play much baseball; they preferred to go to bullfights. Americans, as they still do, knew all about baseball. J. W. Bagby, another psychologist, asked a group of Mexican and American schoolteachers to look into a device that showed a different picture to each eye. One eye saw a bullfighter; the other eye saw a baseball player. When Mexican schoolteachers peered into Bagby's special glasses, they saw a bullfighter. Americans saw the baseball player. Like the people who saw a black ace of spades when they looked at a red card, these teachers saw what they were accustomed to seeing.

Within the past few years, people in the West have begun to realize that other cultures are not wrong, only different. We opened our eyes, discovered that those Indian holy men were not tricking us, and we began to learn. As we learned more about the body, the mind, and the universe, we discovered that the old textbook rules don't cover all the situations in life, and that we weren't nearly as clever twenty years ago as we thought.

Once we admitted we had been wrong about the holy men of India, we realized that we could be wrong about other things as well. Maybe people could read minds or hurl plates through the air with their thoughts or see into the future. Some of us got so excited that we believed every newspaper report of flying dishes and housewives who remembered past lives and young men who bent spoons and started clocks. And that was just as bad as believing none of it.

When we look carefully at the cases in the newspapers, the experiments in the labs, and our everyday experiences we'll see that some of them have nothing to do with parapsychology. Either the story has been garbled or exaggerated, or the incident needs no parapsychology to explain it, or someone has been playing a trick. But we will also find some cases that just can't be explained away. When we encounter those, we should remember the Indian holy men and the red ace of spades.

2

The Missing Motorcyclist

Suppose your thoughts were not private. Suppose each fleeting impulse, each word, each memory that crossed your mind were broadcast for everyone to hear. Walking down the street in such a world would be like walking among a crowd of radios, each tuned to a different station. The thoughts of others would beat upon your mind every minute you were awake.

Life would be very different in that world. It would be impossible to tell lies, but it would also be impossible to stay out of trouble.

In his novel *Mind One,* Mike Dolinsky imagined what would happen in this country if everyone's thoughts suddenly became public. There was no deception in *Mind One.* There was no politeness. There was almost no society. Happy thoughts were drowned out by selfish notions. Every impulse of irritation or anger or contempt or hate, every sexual urge, every memory of an unworthy or shameful act were open to all. Lovers broke up. Fights, riots, and murders filled the streets.

Mind One was science fiction, but it shows why a society of complete mind readers is not likely to evolve. If our early ancestors had had such a free exchange of thoughts, they would have found it difficult to gather in large enough groups to develop a civilization. Those of us who survived might still be living in caves and eating roots we had scratched from the ground with a pointed stick.

The ability to send or receive thoughts is called *telepathy,* and a person who can read minds is a *telepath.* Telepathy is one kind of *extrasensory perception,* or ESP, which means sensing a thought, a person, an object, or an event that ordinary sight, hearing, or touch cannot detect.

Some people believe that our earliest ancestors may have been telepathic, that before they had words to express their wishes, they could use their thoughts. If so, people who could shield their minds from others, keeping their thoughts to themselves, would be more likely to survive and have children who could also keep their thoughts and intentions private.

Gradually, the number of people with tough mind shields increased until all human beings kept their minds shut most of the time. We became nontelepathic. Mind reading still took place, but only under very special conditions that allowed thoughts to penetrate a mind shield.

No one knows if our ancestors could ever read minds. But people often have experiences that convince them that telepathy is real.

Psychologist Gardner Murphy tells about a friend who was driving alone through the night. He was more than six hours from his house in Cedar Rapids, Iowa. As the car sped down the highway, the man became convinced that something was wrong at his home. He felt that he should stop in the town of Dubuque and call his wife.

He had never visited Dubuque, but he knew the name of a large hotel there. He stopped at the hotel to call and discovered a telegram waiting for him. His baby daughter had died, and his wife had wired Dubuque to tell him, even though she had no way of knowing he would stop there.

The man's story is like many other reports of telepathy. It seems as if the wife not only wired the Dubuque hotel, but that she used what Mark Twain called "mental telegraphy" to contact her husband.

There is no way for us to find out if this man was receiving his wife's thoughts and obediently drove to the right hotel in the right town. All we know is what he told Murphy.

People have a tendency to repeat things in a way that leaves out information that might spoil their tale. They also generally make their stories a little better each time they tell them. In this case, we lack a number of facts that would help us to decide whether or not we have just heard about a case of telepathy.

We need to know whether the man often worried about his family and whether he was in the habit of checking on them. If he was a worrier who frequently called home when traveling, then our case of telepathy evaporates. We haven't been told of the many times he worried about his wife and daughter and found that they were safe. Nor have we been told that his wife knew he would be driving through Dubuque, nor whether she contacted more than one hotel in one city.

On the other hand, if the young man never worried, never called home, and his wife had no reason to expect him to be in Dubuque, we must accept the incident as parapsychology. But as it now stands, there is simply not enough information to be certain. The case of the telepathic driver has to be marked "maybe."

Angela von Baillou never received mental messages, but her mother did. In the middle of the night, she shook Angela awake and told her to get up, saying that Angela's brother had been in a motorcycle accident and they must go and find him. "I can see just where he is," the mother said.

Although it was 2 A.M., Angela got out the car and drove her mother along the winding mountain road. Suddenly Mrs. von Baillou told her daughter to stop the car. She then jumped from the car and hurried down the dark mountainside. Angela followed.

There in the brush they found the boy, lying unconscious, his motorcycle on top of him. Again, the story seems convincing. But all we know about this case of telepathy comes from Angela, and she is describing an accident that took place many years ago.

We don't know how much she has forgotten, how much she has added, or how the story has changed over the years. Was her mother a worrier? Did she customarily stay awake until her son came home? Had she expected him to come much earlier? Had she ever dragged Angela out of bed to look for him before? Did he always take the same road home? Was the curve where his motorcycle skidded over the edge the site of many accidents?

The missing or exaggerated facts might make the story seem less miraculous. We just don't know. This case also must be marked "maybe."

One of these stories involves sudden death, the other involves danger. They are like many cases of telepathy. Neither the sender nor the receiver has planned any mental messages. The sender suddenly finds himself dying or in mortal danger, and his thoughts rush across the miles to a close friend or relative.

Such cases are reported so often that it would seem easy enough to check them out. But faced with such a story, the parapsychologist is helpless. He hears about the event weeks or months or even years after it happens. And the people involved are apt to remember few of the details an investigator needs. The emotions surrounding the event have probably changed their memory of the details they can recall.

There is no way to investigate this kind of telepathy. Researchers would have to be on the spot when danger threatens. There is no way to know in advance when a person will be in danger or whether he will try to send a mental message if he is. Nor can a parapsychologist predict which of his friends or relatives a dying person might contact.

Telepathy also seems to occur in everyday situations. Married couples often find themselves seeming to read each other's thoughts.

"We should invite the Andersons over for dinner," the wife says.

"I was just thinking the same thing," her husband answers.

Telepathy? Perhaps. But it is more likely that something they have both just seen or heard or smelled has triggered a memory, the same memory in both their minds.. A husband and wife share many of the same experiences and therefore have many common memories. A car like the one the Andersons drive might have flashed across the TV screen. A voice might have spoken a pet phrase often used by Mrs. Anderson. The man in the next seat on the bus might be smoking Mr. Anderson's brand of pipe tobacco, or a woman might walk by wearing Mrs. Anderson's favorite perfume. Neither the man nor his wife is aware of why either suddenly thought of the Andersons and the overdue dinner invitation.

It is, of course, possible that people who live together for years develop an ability to sense each other's thoughts. But there is no way for a parapsychologist to test this theory. No matter what kind of experiment he devises, all those common memories spoil it. Any proof that telepathy exists will have to come from another source.

For fifty years, parapsychologists have been trying to give us that proof. In 1927, J. B. Rhine began the scientific study of parapsychology at Duke University in North Carolina. He and his associates devised a deck of cards, called Zener cards, to test people for telepathy. Each card had one of five symbols: a circle, a square, a star, a cross, or three wavy lines. There were five cards with each symbol, making a deck of twenty-five.

Using these special cards, Rhine and his associates tested hundreds of people for telepathy. They also tested them for other kinds of parapsychology.

When a person was tested for telepathy, he came into the laboratory and sat down at a table. Sometimes one of the researchers sat across from him. Between them, a screen several feet high divided the table so that the person being tested couldn't see what the researcher was doing. At other times the researcher and the person being tested sat in different rooms.

The researchers shuffled the pack, cut it, and told the person he was ready to begin. One at a time, he turned over a card, looked at the symbol, and concentrated, trying to use his thoughts to send the symbol to the person on the other side of the screen. As the researcher went through the pack, the person being tested wrote down the symbol he thought he was receiving by telepathy.

If no telepathy were involved, a person should make five correct guesses, or "hits," out of twenty-five cards. By pure chance, one out of five guesses should be right.

The laws of chance work in our daily life, too. Suppose your teacher gives you a true-false test of twenty questions. Without even reading the questions, you should be able to guess on ten of them. If you were very lucky, you might get them all. If you were very unlucky, you might miss them all. But if you took one hundred tests, which means you made two thousand guesses, you should have one thousand right answers and one thousand wrong ones.

Rhine found that most people guessed no more cards correctly than the laws of chance said they would. But he found a few people whose guesses were right too often to be accidental. One woman managed to guess an average of seventeen cards correctly, and kept guessing at that rate for three days. What's more, instead of sitting across from the tester, or in the next room, she was two hundred and fifty miles away. It appeared that telepathy did exist.

Whenever one of these telepathic people turned up, Rhine tested him or her again and again. To his dismay, he found that after repeated testing the telepath's scores began to go down. If tested long enough, the telepath did little better than people who had never shown any psychic talent at all. This drop in scores took place no matter what kind of parapsychology was involved.

Some critics said that this loss of telepathic ability only meant that the laws of chance had taken over. If you kept on long enough, they said, you would do no better than chance. Just as your scores on true-false tests would finally average out at half right and half wrong.

Rhine believed that the critics were wrong. Those first scores were too high to be accidents. Telepaths got bored, he said. Or else when people learned they were telepathic, they became afraid and began to miss.

Whatever the reason, potential telepaths always stopped being telepathic. This drop in scores was so reliable that parapsychologists gave it a name. They called the drop the *decline effect,* and there seemed no way to get around it.

3

Seagulls at a Rock Concert

Despite these disappointments, parapsychologists kept working away. Some of them gave up on Zener cards. They decided that Rhine had done all that could be done with the cards and they needed to find some kind of test that would answer their critics.

No matter how convincing a parapsychological experiment seemed, someone always pointed out flaws. Over and over, critics showed how the researcher could influence the results of an experiment. They showed how smiles, nods, and the way a researcher moved could change the answers his subject gave. They showed all the ways that telepaths could cheat and, when their other objections were met, they came right back and hinted that the researcher himself might have cheated.

People were sometimes caught cheating, and that made

the critics' claims seem correct. Glyn and Ieuan Jones, a pair of Welsh teenagers, claimed to have marvelous powers. Their feats of telepathy came to the attention of British parapsychologist S. G. Soal and, in 1955, he decided to test them.

He used decks of cards with various pictures and symbols on them. One boy would try to transmit the picture on a card to his brother. Soal tested the boys when they were together in the same room, when they were in different rooms, when they were outdoors, in every situation he could imagine. No matter where they were, the Jones boys scored high. Once they made twenty-five hits in a row.

Then Soal caught them cheating. The boys had worked out a code that enabled them to signal — by a cough, a sniff, a clearing of the throat — which symbol they were trying to send.

The boys may have always cheated. Or perhaps they began as genuine telepaths. Then, when the decline effect took over and they lost their ESP, they began to cheat. There's no way to tell, but because they did cheat sometimes, we have to assume that they probably cheated all the time.

Machines seemed to be one way of answering the critics. A machine can't smile when a person begins to give the answer it wants, and it can't look excited when an experiment starts to show favorable signs of extrasensory perception.

The first ESP machine was built by G. N. Tyrell in 1938. It consisted of five boxes with lids. Inside each box was a light bulb. The machine lit the bulbs, one at a time, and the telepath opened the lid of the box she thought held the lighted bulb. On a moving paper strip, two pens recorded the telepath's hits and misses.

Tyrell's telepath, Gertrude Johnson, scored far above chance, but people still criticized him. They said that he might be choosing the lights in some sort of pattern and that Johnson had simply figured out part of the pattern. He then invented a mechanical device to select the lights, and Johnson's scores stayed high. But none of the other parapsychologists chose to use Tyrell's box, and gradually the experiments were forgotten.

Other machines were invented, but they were clumsy and hard to use. Besides, as researchers learned how they were influencing their subjects, they changed their experiments so that even they didn't know the answers. Machines were no longer necessary to guard against the clues of smiles and nods.

As time passed, most researchers lost interest in working with people who claimed to be telepaths. None of them seemed to have any control over their powers. They didn't know how they got the right answers, or even when their answers were correct. And in the end there was always the nagging question of the decline effect.

Instead, researchers began to work with groups of people, ordinary people. This seemed to be the only way they would discover just what ESP was and how it worked. If it did. Nearly thirty years went by before parapsychologists would come back again to testing gifted telepaths.

Parapsychologist Charles Tart started the way back when

he decided that most experiments were based on the wrong idea. Researchers spent their time trying to find if people possessed ESP. They would do better, said Tart, if they assumed all people had ESP ability but had to learn to use their power. This meant that parapsychologists had to apply the basic rules of learning to their experiments.

Ever since psychologist B. F. Skinner had figured out some of the rules, psychologists had been teaching pigeons, rats, chimpanzees, and other animals to perform intricate tricks. Skinner had discovered that animals are likely to repeat any act that brings them a reward. A pigeon that gets a grain of corn for pecking a key will peck the key again and again.

Skinner also discovered that a pigeon that has been pecking a key regularly and gobbling up the grains of corn that fall into its cup will keep on pecking when the corn stops falling. But it will peck at the key for only so long. When the pigeon gives up all hope of getting a grain of corn, it stops.

The laws of learning also worked with people. Using these laws, psychologists showed thousands of people how to cure themselves of bad habits. When Tart put learning theory and the decline effect together, he came up with the idea that telepaths stopped being telepathic for the same reason that pigeons stopped pecking keys. They were never rewarded for showing telepathy.

Tart decided that the simplest reward would be to let the telepath know each time he or she made a hit. After all, this kind of reward — called *feedback* — is what helped people learn to play the piano. They could tell at once by the sound of the note whether they had struck the right key.

On the other hand, all the telepaths tested in Rhine's laboratory had no way of knowing when they made a hit. After they had run through twenty-five cards, the tester told them how many hits they had made. It was like putting earmuffs on a piano student and then, after he finished playing a song, saying that he had hit 125 right notes and 75 wrong ones.

The only problem was the one researchers already had been criticized for. When an experimenter plans to tell a telepath if she is right, he often tips her off *before* she gives an answer. Tart decided to let machines do the telling.

He collected twenty-five college students who showed some telepathic ability. In his experiments with them, one of the students sat in front of a machine that showed several unlit light bulbs. In another room sat a sender. An electronic device told the sender which light on the machine would flash next, and he tried to transmit this information to the telepathic student by concentrating on the right answer.

After the student guessed which light would be the next to flash, he pushed a button beside the light he chose. Then the light the sender was trying to send went on, telling the student which of the bulbs had been the target. If he had been right, a chime also rang. At once, the student knew whether he had made a hit. The feedback was as quick as if the student had struck a piano key.

Tart used two machines in his experiment, and he tried to make the guessing as much fun as possible. One machine, called Aquarius, had four lights on its front panel:

one lit up a blue cross, one a yellow square, one a red star, and one a green circle. The other machine had a circle of ten lights; beside each light was the picture of a different playing card.

The fifteen students who tried telepathy on Aquarius did much better at guessing the correct light than they should have. They did so well that there was only one chance in twenty-five hundred that their hits were due to luck.

But students who used telepathy on the ten-light machine dazzled observers. These ten students made five thousand guesses. With luck and without the help of ESP, they should have made five hundred hits. Instead, they guessed the right light 722 times. The odds against that kind of score are 500,000,000,000,000,000,000,000,000 to 1.

The flashing light and the chime after right guesses told students when they made a hit. But not all of the hits were telepathic. Some were due to luck. Students had no way of knowing if their guesses were influenced by mental signals from a sender or if they simply had made a lucky guess.

The students who sat in front of Aquarius had one chance in four of being lucky each time they guessed. The students who used the ten-light machine had only one chance in ten, so they were more likely to get a rewarding chime for showing telepathy, not luck. This difference could explain why the students in the second group did so much better than the students who tackled Aquarius.

Of course, critics could still say that the scorekeeper had cheated. The student who acted as sender kept the records. If he were careless or dishonest, the results would not be accurate. But a computer expert who studied Tart's experiments says that he believes the results show ESP, not cheating. Other researchers, who don't depend on students to keep score, have also shown that feedback fights the decline effect.

So far, feedback hasn't seemed to make a telepath's performance better. No matter how many times the light flashes, most people's scores don't improve. Researchers have rewarded 195 people with feedback. Only 14 of them showed more ESP at the end of the experiments than at the beginning. For the rest, it's as if piano students played no better after ten lessons than after the first. Tart is still trying, but as long as people are rewarded for lucky guesses, feedback is not likely to teach them to pick up information from someone else's mind.

Our failure to learn much about telepathy hasn't killed public interest. In 1970, a rock-and-roll group, the Holy Modal Rounders, turned one of their New York concerts into a telepathy session. Jean Mayo set up a light show and flashed slides and movies of birds on the screen. Many were seagulls, but the show ended with the slide of a phoenix, which appeared then disappeared into a burst of flames. During the light show, the rock group played "If You Want to be a Bird," and the audience was asked to "think birds" and "fly high."

Five people, all within one hundred miles of the concert, sat waiting for a telepathic message. They knew where the concert was being held and the time of the message, but they had no idea what the message would be.

One of the five reported that he got the image of a snake. Another saw a bunch of grapes. Two complete misses.

Parapsychologist Stanley Krippner said he thought of an unborn baby in flames, growing into a tree. Krippner saw the flames but not the birds, which were the main message.

A fourth person said he got a different impression. He saw "something mythological, like a griffin or a phoenix."

Singer Richie Havens closed his eyes. He concentrated and visualized "a number of seagulls flying over water."

If none of the five had had any contact with people who knew about the message being sent, the Holy Modal Rounders reached two telepaths.

4

Tennis Match in a Restaurant

There's more to ESP than telepathy. Even if no one can read minds, someone might be able to tell, without seeing or hearing, what is going on in the next room, the next house, or a thousand miles away. The ability to detect distant events is called *clairvoyance,* or *remote viewing.* Like telepathy, it is usually connected with danger — but not always.

Over a hundred years ago, a young Alabama minister had terrible headaches and convulsions. Afterward, the Reverend Constantine B. Sanders described things he could not have seen and told people to look for lost coins or watches.

Once Sanders claimed that he saw a block of buildings burn in a North Carolina city three hundred miles away. He was right. Another time he seemed upset and suddenly said, "Poor fellow! How he suffers! He is almost gone! He is going! Going! Gone!" Sanders had just seen the death of a neighbor who was visiting in Tennessee. Sure enough, the next day the young man's fiancée got a telegram reporting her sweetheart's death.

We know about Sanders because of a book published in 1876. The book listed seventy witnesses who had seen Sanders perform his clairvoyant feats. Everyone involved in the case is dead; there's no way to investigate it. We'll never know if the book was a hoax or the story of an amazing clairvoyant.

It's often hard to separate clairvoyance from telepathy. The woman who dashed out into the middle of the night to find her son pinned under a motorcycle might have picked up her information from telepathy, from clairvoyance, or from a combination of the two. These varieties of ESP are so closely linked that some parapsychologists call them GESP, short for General ESP, which means either telepathy or clairvoyance.

The case of a young man in Dallas, Texas, could be either. This man came home from teaching an amateur astronomy class and sat on the edge of his bed. Suddenly his father, who was supposed to be in California, appeared in the room. He was dressed in work clothes, with a cloth cap on his head and a caliper rule in his shirt pocket. When the young man spoke, the figure disappeared.

At that moment a telegram arrived. The man's father had just died in California. He had been working on the car that day, and on a chair beside his bed lay his work clothes, cloth cap, and rule. If we call this incident GESP, we don't have to decide whether it was a telepathic call from a dying man or a case of clairvoyance. Of course, we have no way of knowing if the death visit actually took place. No one was with the young man when it happened. Like all such incidents, this case is a "maybe."

Many people have small experiences that seem clairvoyant. Perhaps you suddenly think of a friend who lives in another city. That same day you get a letter from her. You may have been clairvoyant, but there could be another explanation. Your friend might be a slow correspondent who generally waits about two months to answer your letters. It's been two months since you last wrote her and, although you didn't consciously expect a letter, you were somehow aware that one was due. The answer could be even simpler. You may have thought of your friend at several different times without getting a letter. Hearing from your friend on a day when you remembered her was pure chance.

All the problems that go with checking out cases of telepathy apply to clairvoyance. When researchers first studied clairvoyance in Rhine's lab, they used the Zener cards. But no sender turned over the cards and tried to send mental messages to the person being tested. Instead, the clairvoyant went through the pack and, keeping the cards face down, called out the symbol he thought was on the face of each card. After he ran through the deck, the cards were turned over and his guesses checked against the actual order of the cards.

The best-known clairvoyant studied by Rhine was Hubert Pearce. Once when Rhine was running through the

Zener deck with Pearce, he bet the clairvoyant one hundred dollars that he couldn't guess all the cards. Pearce called all twenty-five correctly.

In 1933, parapsychologist J. Gaither Pratt set up a series of experiments with Pearce. The clairvoyant was in one building and Pratt in another. Pearce tried to guess 1850 cards and was right 558 times. Lucky guesses could account for 370 of his hits, but the odds are 22 thousand million to 1 that luck was responsible for all 558 hits.

The Pearce-Pratt experiments have not been accepted by everyone. One critic, C. E. M. Hansel, said that either Pearce had an accomplice who helped him cheat or else he sneaked across to Pratt's building, peeked through a transom, and copied down some of the cards as Pratt turned them over. But another parapsychologist, Ian Stevenson, visited both buildings and said that it was impossible to see through the transom to the desk where Pratt sat.

With Hubert Pearce, Rhine thought he finally had found a subject who would not show the decline effect. Pearce was good at all kinds of ESP. His score dipped when a stranger came to watch him at work, but it always rose again when he got used to the visitor. Then Pearce had a disappointment in love. His psi ability completely disappeared. He became a Methodist minister. Although he tried again and again, his ESP never came back.

One clairvoyant who has held on to his ability for a long time is Pavel Stepanek, a Czech. Stepanek can do only one thing: guess the color of a card that is inside a sealed envelope. Researchers put a card into a cardboard envelope, then put each envelope inside a heavy cardboard cover.

Stepanek must look at the cardboard cover and guess whether the card inside has its green or white side turned toward him. He has made thousands and thousands of guesses and generally guesses right about fifty-five times out of every one hundred tries. By chance, he should be right fifty times. Those five extra guesses wouldn't mean much in a hundred tries, but the odds against keeping that average for more than ten years are half a million to one.

This Czech clairvoyant has been tested in his own country by Czech, Dutch, and American parapsychologists. He has also come to the United States, where Pratt tested him at Rhine's laboratory. Researchers have discovered that Stepanek seems to home in on certain envelopes. When these envelopes turn up inside the cardboard covers, he hits almost every time. Yet neither Stepanek nor the researchers testing him know which envelope is inside a particular cover. On other envelopes, he does no better than you or I would do. Parapsychologists are still trying to figure out why.

The latest news on Stepanek is not good. His score has slowly begun to slip. Apparently he has at last run into the decline effect.

A different kind of clairvoyance is being studied at the Stanford Research Institute in California. Russell Targ and Harold Puthoff found that Pat Price, a former police commissioner, could "see" objects at a distance. In remote-viewing tests with Price, a research team opened a sealed envelope, took out a paper that described a trip to some building or landmark in the San Francisco Bay area, and drove to it. When the team arrived at the chosen site, they signaled the lab by walkie-talkie, and Price tried to describe the place and tell what was happening there. The researchers who stayed with Price and taped his comments did not know where the team had gone.

The team visited nine sites, and Price described each of them. Sometimes he seemed to be seeing parts of the landscape around the team: buildings, roads, gardens. At other times his descriptions were entirely wrong.

Five judges, who were not connected with the research, tried to match Price's statements with the nine places. Every judge agreed that Price had hit with his description of Hoover Tower, a building on the Stanford University campus. None of the judges could identify his description of the toll booths at a bridge, and only one judge recognized his description of a drive-in theater. But a majority of the five judges recognized five of the nine sites from Price's account, and one judge matched seven.

Targ and Puthoff say that they have found other people who seem to have this kind of clairvoyance, and they believe almost anyone can develop it. When psychologist Robert Ornstein examined their experiments, he discovered an odd thing. One man, asked to draw a remote site, drew a picture that closely resembled the tennis match the research team was visiting. Judges would say he had made a hit. But when the man tried to describe what he saw, he said that the team was visiting a crowded restaurant. His picture was accurate, but he did not know what he had "seen."

Once again, researchers have run into a wall. People who seem to have an ability to gather information by paranormal channels don't know what they have or how to use it.

PART TWO

Precognition

"It's a poor sort of memory that only works backward," the Queen remarked.

Lewis Carroll,
Through the Looking-Glass

5

A Single Red Rose

Mark Twain once woke from a frightening dream: his brother Henry lay dead in a metal coffin, which rested on two chairs. On his chest was a bouquet of white flowers with a single red rose in its center. The dream seemed so real to the author of *Tom Sawyer* that he got up and dressed, intending to go see his brother's body, which he believed lay in the next room.

Twain's grief led him to postpone the visit. Instead, he went for a solitary walk. He had covered nearly a block before he realized that he had only dreamed of his brother's death. When Twain got back to the house, he told his sister about the dream.

Henry Clemens, Twain's brother, worked on a Mississippi riverboat. Several weeks after Twain's dream, the boilers on Henry's boat, *Pennsylvania*, blew up. Within a few days, Henry died from his injuries. Twain went to see his brother's body. It lay in a metal coffin, which rested on two chairs. As Twain watched, a woman entered, went over to the coffin, and placed a bouquet of flowers on Henry's chest. The flowers were all white except for a single red rose in their center.

Mark Twain had experienced a kind of extrasensory perception that is called *precognition,* which means "to know before." People who have such precognitive dreams seem somehow to have grasped a bit of information from the future.

In Twain's case, our first impulse is to dismiss the dream as the result of an anxious brother's fears. After all, riverboats blew up frequently and Twain, who had worked on the boats himself, knew the danger. The threat of exploding boilers hung over riverboats, just as the threat of a crash haunts airplanes.

But Twain's dream has one element that seems to stretch coincidence: the bouquet of flowers. If the flowers were not later brilliant embroidery by a master storyteller, but were part of Twain's telling of the dream that first morning, we have to accept it as a case of precognition.

Other famous people have had similar dreams. Three weeks before he was assassinated, Abraham Lincoln had a dream that disturbed him. One of the people who heard his account of it wrote down Lincoln's words:

> There seemed to be a deathlike stillness about me. Then I heard subdued sobs, as if a number of people were weeping. I thought I left my bed and wandered downstairs. There the silence was broken by

the same pitiful sobbing, but the mourners were invisible. I went from room to room. No living person was in sight, but the same mournful sounds of distress met me as I passed along. It was light in all the rooms; every object was familiar to me, but where were all the people who were grieving as if their hearts would break? I was puzzled and alarmed. What could be the meaning of all this? Determined to find the cause of a state of affairs so mysterious and shocking, I kept on until I arrived in the East Room, which I entered. There I met with a sickening surprise. Before me was a catafalque, on which rested a corpse in funeral vestments. Around it were stationed soldiers who were acting as guards; and there was a throng of people, some gazing mournfully upon the corpse, whose face was covered, others weeping pitifully. "Who is dead in the White House?" I demanded of one of the soldiers. "The President," was his answer. "He was killed by an assassin."

Lincoln's dream may indeed have been precognitive. We know, however, that he expected to die soon. He once told Harriet Beecher Stowe, the author of *Uncle Tom's Cabin*, "Whichever way the War ends, I have the impression I shall not last long after it is over." We also know that Lincoln was the target of abuse from Southerners and Northerners alike. He received threatening letters nearly every day. There is no way to know whether his dream was truly a glimpse of the future or his own reaction to continual threats against his life.

The death of another President was preceded by what

at first appears to be a precognitive vision. In April 1962, parapsychologist Stanley Krippner took the drug psilocybin. While under its influence, he seemed to be standing in the White House, looking at a bust of Lincoln. Then he noticed a gun at the base of the statue. A wisp of smoke emerged from the barrel and someone whispered, "He was shot. The President was shot." As the words were repeated, Lincoln's features faded and the bust became a statue of John F. Kennedy. As soon as the drug wore off, Krippner told people about his vision.

Less than two years later, President Kennedy was assassinated as he rode down the streets of Dallas. People who do not remember the 1960 election are likely to point to Krippner's vision as an instance of precognition. But during that election year, newspapers were full of stories about the deaths of presidents. Again and again, people read that since 1840, every U.S. President elected at twenty-year intervals had died in office. William Henry Harrison, elected in 1840, died of pneumonia. Abraham Lincoln, elected in 1860, was assassinated. James A. Garfield, elected in 1880, was assassinated. William McKinley, elected in 1900, was assassinated. Warren Harding, elected in 1920, died in office. Franklin Delano Roosevelt, elected in 1940, died in office — although he lived to complete that term and died only after he had been elected to the presidency for a fourth time.

Krippner himself doubts that the vision was precognitive. When he was ten years old, he had discovered the apparent twenty-year cycle of presidential deaths and studied it closely. At that time, Roosevelt had been elected for his third term, and Krippner must have wondered if the

President would live to complete it. Krippner also saw the articles that appeared during the 1960 campaign. It is probable that when the parapsychologist took psilocybin, his boyhood memories, which had been strengthened by the campaign publicity, came flooding back and influenced his vision.

Some people say that precognition has saved their lives. Aniela Jaffe, who worked with the great psychoanalyst Carl Jung, collected such stories. The vision is not always clear. Jaffe tells about the mother who was getting ready to take her seven-year-old son on a skiing trip. The pair was ready to leave the house when the mother suddenly felt that they must not go. The weather reports were good, the boy had looked forward to the expedition. There seemed no reason to stay home. But the mother's feeling became so strong that she canceled the trip.

That night news came over the radio of a terrible train accident. As the mother listened, she realized that the wrecked train was the one they would have taken home from the ski slopes.

Ian Stevenson, a parapsychologist at the University of Virginia, studied the sinking of the ocean liner *Titanic*. The *Titanic* was believed to be unsinkable. She had been carefully built with a double bottom and watertight compartments. Her builders were so sure that their beautiful ship could not sink that they gave her only a few lifeboats. On her maiden voyage across the Atlantic in 1912, the great liner struck an iceberg and sank rapidly. Because there was no room for them in the lifeboats, fifteen hundred people drowned.

One man who should have been on the *Titanic* was Colin

Macdonald, a marine engineer. Macdonald had made many crossings in transatlantic ships, and he was offered the job of second engineer on the new *Titanic*. Normally, he would have jumped at the chance. The post as second-in-command of the ship's engines and power plants was a promotion. But Macdonald said he had a hunch that he should not sail on the *Titanic*. Three times he was offered the post, and three times he turned it down. The man who sailed in his place drowned with the ship.

J. Connon Middleton was also supposed to be on the *Titanic*. Middleton was an English businessman who bought a ticket for the *Titanic's* first voyage. About ten days before the ship sailed, he had a disturbing dream. The *Titanic* was "floating on the sea, keel upwards, and her passengers and crew were swimming around her." The next night he dreamed the same dream. By this time he was uneasy, but he did not cancel his passage until he got a cable from the U.S. saying that the business he was to transact there had been postponed for a few days.

Before the ship sailed, Middleton told his family and friends about the dream. The dream was wrong in its details of the sinking and, by itself, did not make Middleton cancel his ticket. But it is possible that without it, he might have gone ahead with his plans to sail on the maiden voyage of the world's largest liner.

The Marshalls never planned to sail on the *Titanic*. They lived on the Isle of Wight, which lay near the *Titanic's* course. When the big ship steamed out of Southampton and past the island, the Marshalls were watching from the roof of their home. As they watched the liner go by,

Mrs. Marshall suddenly became upset. She grabbed her husband's arm and said, "That ship is going to sink before she reaches America."

Both her husband and her friends tried to calm her, explaining that the *Titanic* was unsinkable. The builders had said so. None of their soothing words had any effect. At last Mrs. Marshall exclaimed, "Don't stand there staring at me! Do something! You fools, I can see hundreds of people struggling in the icy water! Are you all so blind that you are going to let them drown?" Four days later the ship struck the iceberg.

Stevenson found nineteen different cases of ESP connected with the *Titanic*'s sinking. Some were precognitive. Others were either clairvoyant or telepathic.

One woman awoke in New York from a terrible dream. She had seen her mother in a crowded lifeboat in the middle of the ocean. The boat was so packed with people that it looked as if it would soon sink beneath the waters. Her husband tried to soothe her, pointing out that her mother was safe in England. But his words did no good. She had not just had a bad dream, she insisted. "It was something so awful — frightening and all so real."

It *was* real. Her mother had sailed on the *Titanic*, planning to surprise her daughter. At the time her daughter had the terrifying dream, the mother was seated in an overcrowded lifeboat, thinking that she would never again see her daughter.

As with other kinds of ESP, precognition is nearly impossible to prove. People tend to forget premonitions of events that never take place and remember only those that come true. Many people may have dreamed that other ocean liners, ships that safely crossed the sea, were doomed to sink. In the days before radar, a North Atlantic crossing was a risky business, and ships had to keep watch for icebergs. The builders' insistence that the *Titanic* was unsinkable may have reminded people of this danger and caused them to dream about a possible disaster. Warnings of assassination, train wrecks, plane crashes, and other disasters are usually written down only after the tragedy occurs, and thus cannot be accepted as solid evidence.

Parapsychologist W. E. Cox's investigation of railway accidents indicates that premonitions of disaster may be more widespread than we realize. He studied twenty-eight train wrecks, checking the records of railway travel for seven days before and a few days after each accident. He found that trains traveling on the day of an accident carried noticeably fewer passengers than trains traveling before or after the fatal day. He also found that damaged and derailed coaches held a smaller than normal load of passengers.

Cox believes that many people get some kind of warning of disaster, but do not recognize it as precognition. They switch their travel plans without realizing that they are responding to a precognitive warning.

Cox's study cannot be considered proof, and his findings do not convince skeptics. But reports like those in this chapter have led to the establishment of several agencies that are trying to collect information on precognition.

In England, the British Premonitions Bureau was set up in 1967. When Andrew MacKenzie checked six years of the Bureau's records, he found over twelve hundred reports. Some of the cases are interesting, such as the prediction recorded on November 21, 1968, that a number of young children would panic, rush to the end of a room, and die there. Four days later, at Beauvais, France, fourteen children died in a fire at a home for mentally retarded children. But the prediction spoke of no flames and could easily have been coincidence. None of the cases presented by MacKenzie has the kind of detail that made Mark Twain's dream of his brother's death so convincing.

Perhaps similar research in this country will one day settle the question. The Central Premonitions Registry in New York City and the Premonitions Registry Bureau in Berkeley, California, are collecting predictions.

More than three thousand people have sent premonitions to the New York registry, some of them reporting at least one prediction each week. About forty were followed by events that seem to fulfill the predictions, and over half occurred in dreams. Many, such as picking a World Series winner, could easily be lucky guesses. Others, such as foretelling the death by heart attack of Egyptian ruler Gamal Abdel Nasser, seem convincing. Even more convincing is the fact that five people produced nearly half the hits.

But a word of caution. Reports do not tell us how detailed those predictions were, nor how many misses the precognitive five registered. It will be a long time before we find out if precognitive warnings are anything more than the uneasy feeling each air traveler experiences before he undertakes a flight.

6

The Spin of the Wheel

From the beginning of recorded history, humankind has tried to peer into the future. Oracles, soothsayers, and astrologers claimed they could see events before they happened. Today, fortunetellers and psychics say they have the same precognitive talent. They make their livings by predicting for pay and often point with pride to their successful predictions.

Psychics are as likely as the rest of us to remember only their successes. Thelma Moss, a parapsychologist at the University of California at Los Angeles, kept track of several famous psychics for three years. She disregarded prophecies that were guaranteed to come true, those that were so vague that they could not miss. When, for example, a psychic predicts that during the next year there will be an earthquake in California, he can't miss. Every year there are earthquakes in California. Such prophecies are no riskier than predicting that Christmas will fall on December 25.

Instead, Moss kept track of specific prophecies, such as "An epidemic of smallpox will break out in Uruguay in May and thousands will perish." If the psychic who predicted a California earthquake had said, "In April an earthquake will be centered in Bakersfield, California, and several people will die," his earthquake prediction would have been counted.

At the end of three years, Moss tallied the psychics' scores. Less than 5 percent of their specific predictions came to pass. That means that out of every one hundred predictions the psychics made, more than ninety-five were wrong.

In July 1976, the *National Enquirer* published the predictions of ten psychics for the last half of 1976. Five of them correctly forecast Jimmy Carter's election as President, and one said that an apparent FBI cover-up would lead to a new investigation of President Kennedy's assassination. Either prediction might have been made by an average newspaper reader.

Most of the forecasts, however, were just plain wrong. President Ford did not push through a major tax cut just before the election. An eastbound 747 jet did not crash in October, killing several top movie stars. Three U.S. senators were not arrested on charges of spying for Russia. Frank Sinatra did not knock a gun from an assassin's hand, and save a politician's life. Lucille Ball did not become a U.S. ambassador to an Asian nation. Israel was not wiped out in one of the bloodiest wars in history. Murderer Charles Manson did not escape from prison. Fidel Castro was not ousted as Premier of Cuba. Prince Charles of England was not temporarily lost at sea. The CIA did not reveal that it had discovered how to make objects vanish and then reappear. A gigantic earthquake did not tear apart California mountain ranges, revealing the biggest gold deposit ever discovered. Space probes did not reveal evidence of ancient civilizations on Mars. An Air Force jet did not crash in October after encountering a UFO, and Earth did not receive a message from a civilization in outer space.

The *National Enquirer*'s psychics did no better than those studied by Thelma Moss. But chances are that the five who foretold Carter's election will remind people of their success and conveniently forget about their long lists of misses.

Watching the predictions of psychics is not the only way to study precognition. It was not difficult for parapsychologists to design tests of precognition. A person simply had to guess the order of the cards in the Zener pack before the deck was shuffled. His or her guesses were recorded, the pack was shuffled and cut, and the cards turned over one at a time.

But studies of precognition ran into the same problems that other ESP studies encountered. After a series of tests, people who seemed to know how the cards would fall after the next shuffle ran into the decline effect. They would begin to average five hits on each run and never regain their power.

Some tests of precognition gave feedback to the people who tried to see the future. Helmut Schmidt, a physicist who studies parapsychology at Rhine's North Carolina institute, invented a machine that resembled the Aquarius tester used by Tart. The person being tested pressed a button beside the light he thought would flash next, but in this test, his choice was made before the machine knew which target light would flash.

Because no one can read an atom's mind, Schmidt let strontium 90 pick the light. When a radioactive element decays, it throws off electrons at irregular intervals. Not even a nuclear physicist can determine precisely when the element will throw off its next electron. Schmidt placed a piece of strontium 90 inside his tester and let its decaying electrons choose the target light.

Within the tester, an electronic switch moved rapidly among the four positions that matched the lights on the front of the machine. When the person being tested pressed a button on the machine's panel, a gate opened between the switch and a Geiger counter. With the gate open, the next electron from the decaying strontium 90 that struck the switch turned on the light that matched the switch's position.

When Schmidt tested several people who had shown some ESP talent, there was no decline effect. Their ability to outguess the electrons held up through more than twenty thousand trials.

Schmidt's machine acted as a teacher with one subject. B. D.'s first test on the machine showed strong signs of precognition. Then the researchers, E. Kelly and H. Kanthamani, connected a recording device to the Schmidt machine. As soon as the device, which punched the results of B. D.'s test into a strip of tape, was attached to the machine, B. D.'s score dropped almost to chance. B. D. refused to quit. He worked at the machine for eight days and managed, with the help of feedback, to get his score close to his original rate of precognition.

In a test with another machine, a young girl learned to predict the future without ever knowing she was being tested for precognition. The girl was hitting well above chance on tests for clairvoyance, in which the targets were picked before she made her guesses. After she had made more than fifteen hundred guesses, Russell Targ and D. Hurt rewired the machine so that the targets were selected *after* she chose a light. The test was now one of precognition.

The girl began to guess, then stopped. She said she no longer felt anything. She was "just guessing." Her score fell until it reached the level of chance. She kept working at the machine, however, and her score climbed. More than six hundred guesses later, she showed strong evidence of precognition. Feedback had again been a silent teacher.

Unfortunately, none of these experiments are perfect. We can't tell from Targ and Hurt's description of the girl's performance whether she was watched by an experimenter. Charles Tart's son discovered that he could cheat on a similar machine, raising his score by one hit in each run of twenty-four guesses. And other parapsychologists have used Schmidt's machine without getting the same positive results.

What is more, none of these talented people has enough control over his or her abilities to be reliable forecasters. The psychic girl who switched from clairvoyance to precognition still missed 1078 times out of 1536 tries, and on her last 96 guesses, missed 58 times.

One way to put precognition to practical use would be in games of chance. Robert Brier and Walter Tyminski decided to find out if someone who scored well on tests of precognition could make money in a gambling casino. American roulette wheels have eighteen black numbers, eighteen red numbers, and two green numbers. Players who want to bet on a color may choose either red or black. In twenty-five spins of the wheel, a player with no ability to predict the future should be able to guess right just under twelve times (11.84).

H. B., who had done well on other tests, made a series of guesses for Brier and Tyminski, predicting whether the roulette wheel would stop on red or on black. The pair of researchers took her guesses to the casino and checked her first twenty-five predictions against the spin of the wheel. If H. B. made thirteen or more hits, they would bet on her next twenty-five guesses. If she were wrong fourteen or more times, they would bet against her. If she had twelve hits, they would not bet.

H. B. was right thirteen times, just slightly better than chance. Brier and Tyminski bet H. B.'s predictions on the next twenty-five spins of the wheel and won handsomely. She had guessed right eighteen times.

The following night, Brier and Tyminski returned to the casino with another set of fifty predictions. Again they

checked the first twenty-five spins and discovered that
H. B. was right fifteen times. They bet on the next twenty-
five turns of the wheel and won thirteen times, only once
above chance, but enough to give them a slight profit for
the evening.

The third day they went to the casino in the afternoon.
This time H. B.'s first twenty-five guesses turned up only
twelve hits. The researchers made no bets. As it turned
out, they should have bet against H. B. She was right only
ten times on the next twenty-five spins.

That evening Brier and Tyminski made another try.
H. B.'s first twenty-five guesses were right at chance, and so
were the next twenty-five. Again, they placed no bets. At
the end of their experiment, the parapsychologists were
ahead, but most of their profit had come from the first
night. The casino lost to precognition on the first two visits,
then stopped losing.

Brier and Tyminski quit trying to beat the roulette
wheel. Their seer had met the decline effect and lost. Because they stopped their experiment, we'll never know if
H. B. would have regained her powers or whether her
guesses for the first two nights were merely lucky.

PART THREE

Psychokinesis

"Things flow about so here!" she said at last in a plaintive tone, after she had spent a minute or so in vainly pursuing a large bright thing, that looked sometimes like a doll and sometimes like a work-box, and was always in the shelf next above the one she was looking at. "And this one is the most provoking of all — but I'll tell you what —" she added, as a sudden thought struck her. "I'll follow it up to the very top shelf of all. It'll puzzle it to go through the ceiling, I expect!"

But even this plan failed: the "thing" went through the ceiling as quietly as possible, as if it were quite used to it.

Lewis Carroll,
Through the Looking-Glass

7

Grandfather's Clock

A clock stops at the moment a woman dies. Twelve months later, exactly one year to the minute since that event, the clock stops again. Three years later the clock stops when a grandchild is born, and yet again when a member of the family is married. This clock, which belongs to a family in Illinois, resembles the one in the familiar song:

My grandfather's clock was too large for the shelf,
So it stood ninety years on the floor;
It was taller by half than the old man himself,
Tho' it weighed not a pennyweight more.
It was bought on the morn of the day that he was born,
And was always his treasure and pride;
But it stopped short, never to go again,
When the old man died.

J. B. Rhine once called *My Grandfather's Clock* "a good old parapsychological song." The clock in the song and the clock in Illinois both stopped because of yet another kind of parapsychology: *psychokinesis*, or PK. Psychokinesis means "mind-movement" and describes the ability to move or change an object, plant, animal, or person merely by willing it to happen. PK is not ESP, for ESP refers only to the ability to become aware of thoughts, objects, or events. PK always refers to actions.

We don't know if the clock in Illinois stopped because it broke or because the daughter of the dying woman willed it to do so. Louisa Rhine, who got a letter describing the clock's antics, believes the daughter did it. If so, she used PK without being aware of it.

It might be pleasant to have such power. You could command the refrigerator door to open and will a can of cola to fly across the room and land in your waiting hand. Or, when you tired of watching Columbo apologize for bothering a murderer, you could concentrate for a moment and your TV set would obediently switch channels. Or suppose your arms were loaded with packages and you came to a locked door. A touch of PK and the door would swing open like the cavern that responded to Ali Baba's cry of "Open, Sesame!"

But that's not the way PK usually shows itself. For years the Rhines have collected reports of incidents that sound like PK. Most of their stories come from people who have had peculiar things happen to them, things they just can't explain. Many of these stories occur at times of death or danger. The picture of a young sailor falls from the wall of his home when his ship sinks, carrying him to the bottom of the sea. When a marriage breaks up, a vase that was a prized wedding present suddenly shatters. A man dies, and both the watch in his pocket and the clock in his bedroom stop.

Because these stories describe things that have already happened, there is never any way for the Rhines to investigate them. Some may have natural causes, some may be imagination, some may be hoaxes, but some may also be real.

There is a kind of PK that can be investigated. This sort of psychokinesis doesn't stop with one incident, but goes on for weeks, or even months. Parapsychologists generally discover such a case by reading stories in the newspapers about a house that seems bewitched. Strange thuds and bangs echo through the rooms, plates fly from the shelves, corks pop out of bottles, lights go on and off, doors swing open, stones fall onto roofs.

Reporters usually say that such events are the work of *poltergeists,* which is German for "noisy ghosts," because ghosts are often the first explanation people give for things they can't explain. Parapsychologists prefer to call such hauntings *recurrent spontaneous psychokinesis,* or RSPK, which is a way of saying that the PK happens again and again all by itself, without anyone appearing to direct it.

People have written about RSPK for centuries. When Hereward Carrington combed the records, he found five cases that took place before the year 1000. These ancient poltergeists rapped on walls, made stones shower from the heavens, started fires, and flung objects around the room.

Through the years, cases of RSPK came from Great Britain, France, the United States, Germany, Scandinavia, Africa, China, Java, South America, Jamaica, and Haiti.

For centuries, RSPK was thought to be the work of the devil. The strange events usually centered about one person. Whenever that person left the building, the noises, stones, and flying cups and plates stopped. Such a person was believed to be possessed by a demon, and the church often sent priests to exorcise, or expel, the evil spirit.

Priests still get asked to exorcise demons. The movie *The Exorcist* was based on a case that happened in 1949, except that the person who was supposed to be possessed was not a girl, but a thirteen-year-old boy who lived in Washington, D.C.

It all began with what seemed like an infestation of rodents. Scratching noises came from the walls. An exterminator could find no traces of rats or mice. Then ghostly footsteps were heard, dishes flew about, furniture began to move by itself, and the boy's bed shook and trembled. Wherever he went — to school, to a friend's, to the neighbor's — the strange events followed.

His parents decided their son was possessed and asked their minister to help them. Prayers didn't help. Neither did visits to a mental health clinic. The minister wrote Rhine's laboratory. It was not until after the son had been taken to St. Louis, where a Lutheran minister, an Episcopal priest, and two Roman Catholic priests spent thirty-five days attempting to cast out his demons that any symptoms of "possession" appeared.

After the boy had been told again and again by his

family and the clergymen that he was in the spell of the devil, he began to attack adults, vomit, spit in the exorcist's eye, and go into convulsions. Almost two months after the exorcism began, the symptoms disappeared. They have never returned and, now grown and married, he leads a normal life.

Parapsychologist J. Gaither Pratt reports that the case seemed a clear example of RSPK. Pratt believes that the boy was never possessed. He says that the strange behavior in St. Louis was probably the result of the attempted exorcism. The boy had heard so often that he had a demon within him that he believed it and began to behave the way the priests expected him to behave. Pratt says that, far from ending the boy's troubles, the exorcism probably prolonged it. He believes that the symptoms would have disappeared much earlier if the boy had been left alone.

The case of *The Exorcist* is typical of RSPK in another way. The poltergeist activity came from an adolescent. In almost every reported case of RSPK, the disturbances come from a boy or girl who is between ten and nineteen years old. The unlucky teenager generally seems calm on the outside, but inside he or she is upset, hostile, and anxious. Parapsychologists like Pratt believe that, instead of exploding with anger, the teenager lets off steam by causing the strange noises and sending objects bounding about. But, Pratt says, the boy or girl does not plan the strange events and even doesn't know how they happen.

Not everyone accepts Pratt's explanation. Critics agree that RSPK is often the work of a disturbed teenager, but they say that the whole thing is a case of malicious mischief. The adolescent uses tricks to accomplish his feats: pulling objects off shelves by means of strings or placing cups and vases near the edge, where heavy footsteps will tip them over.

Sometimes the critics are right. Some cases are frauds from the beginning. Poltergeists are often caught in the act. A few years ago in Pursruck, West Germany, a pair of sisters became the center of RSPK. Hammerings, bumps, scrapes, and bangs came from beds, cupboards, and doors in their home. The sounds went on for three weeks, stopped for six months, then started up again. When the girls were watched carefully, thirteen-year-old Helga and eleven-year-old Anna were caught knocking against the bedstead with their fingers and toes.

Hans Bender, whose Freiburg Institute has investigated more than thirty-five reported poltergeists since World War II, discovered the girls' trickery. He believes that real cases of RSPK sometimes wind up in such mischief and that Helga and Anna might have shown RSPK in the beginning.

Most poltergeists have a fairly short existence. A few weeks of crashing crockery and thumping sounds and the disturbances cease. RSPK seems to let out the adolescent's anger and ease his or her tensions, just as a few good arguments clear the air. When parapsychologists are called in to investigate, they bring cameras and tape recorders and spend hours at a time waiting for a stone to fall, a table to move, a vase to drop. As the researchers grow impatient, the angry young person who has been causing the disturbances obliges them, perhaps by picking up a rock and throwing it at a window.

Sometimes poltergeists turn out to be no more than rats in the walls, the settling of an old house, underground water, or some other natural cause that has nothing to do with RSPK. But sometimes no explanation can be found.

When a lawyer's office in Rosenheim, West Germany, was plagued by a poltergeist, light bulbs exploded, neon tubes unscrewed themselves, chandeliers swung, fuses blew, and telephones dialed and rang by themselves. Besides being annoying, this poltergeist was expensive. The lawyer's telephone bills soared. One phone, by itself, dialed the local post office over and over again, as often as six times a minute.

The news leaked out, television crews came in, and all of West Germany learned of the mysterious events. Someone suspected that surges of power in the electricity supply were causing the trouble. An automatic recording device, installed by the power company, showed wild fluctuations. But a second instrument, installed and checked by two physicists from the Max Planck Institute in Munich, showed that the power supply to the building did not vary. Both recorders checked out perfectly in the laboratory. The physicists threw up their hands and said that the disturbances must be "intelligently controlled."

Parapsychologists from the Freiburg Institute soon found that Annemarie, a nineteen-year-old secretary, was the center of activity. When she was out of the office, everything was normal. As soon as the trouble was labeled RSPK, things got worse. Paintings swung on the walls, drawers slid open, and a large filing cabinet twice moved away from the wall. Annemarie began to have spasms in her arms and legs.

When the young woman quit her job and went to work for another company, the poltergeist stopped bothering the lawyer. But at Annemarie's new office, RSPK began, this time on a small scale. The incidents were kept out of the paper. Gradually, with no publicity to encourage them, the disturbances ended.

It is cases like Annemarie's that make it hard to explain away RSPK. The best efforts of electronic detectors, cameras, tape recorders, the post office, the local power company, the police, telephone company engineers, physicists, and parapsychologists could neither find a natural explanation nor catch Annemarie cheating. The German secretary seems to have shown a genuine burst of RSPK.

8

The Ping-Pong Ball

On at least one occasion, parapsychologists have brought poltergeists into the laboratory. In 1967, a Miami novelty company was plagued by RSPK. A team of parapsychologists came to Florida from Rhine's North Carolina Institute. They found that the crashing beer mugs, the cascading boxes of back scratchers and pencil sharpeners were the work of Julio Vasquez, a nineteen-year-old Cuban refugee. Julio did not seem to know that he was the poltergeist. But he did feel better after a glass fell from a shelf or a box overturned. Once he said, "That made me feel good."

William Roll, one of the researchers, took Julio back to North Carolina and tested him at the Institute. A medical examination turned up nothing. A recording of his brain waves was normal. Psychological tests revealed that he was an unhappy young man. He missed his mother and grandmother, whom he had left behind in Cuba, and he believed that his work as a shipping clerk was far beneath him. He showed no signs of ESP, and his scores on tests for PK showed only a slight talent. But strange things happened.

Roll used dice to test Julio's powers of PK. The dice were kept in a mesh cage and shaken by an electric motor. The person being tested never touched the dice, but he tried to make them fall with certain combinations showing. Most of the time Julio did no better than you or I would do.

But sometimes the four spring latches that locked the cage sprang open and the dice tumbled onto the floor. When this happened, Julio's score went up. The rolling dice often stopped to show the faces he had been concentrating on. Never before had the latches opened during an experiment.

What is more, about an hour after Julio entered the laboratory, a large decorative bottle that stood on a table about sixteen feet from him tumbled off and broke. At the time, Julio was standing in the doorway with a cup in his hand, and two parapsychologists could see all of him except for his left arm and shoulder. Because they could not see all of him, the researchers say that Julio may have used trickery instead of RSPK to break the bottle, but they doubt it. The parapsychologists believe that they had a case of RSPK on their hands.

Dice are one of the usual ways parapsychologists test people who claim to have PK. Rhine first used them in 1934, when a young gambler told him that he could win money at craps by using his mind to direct the fall of the dice; he could, far more often than the law of chance would predict.

In one experiment, a group of divinity students, who tried to influence the dice by prayer, competed against a group of the "best crap shooters on campus," who presumably used PK to help them win. The Rhines set up the contest. It ended in a tie, but both groups beat the averages; their scores were above chance.

W. E. Cox tried a different kind of experiment with dice. He asked people to make the dice stop rolling in a certain place, paying no attention to the number that showed. Cox marked off the inside of a typewriter case in 252 squares and marked each square with a number from one to six. The job of the person being tested was to choose a number and then make as many of the dice as possible stop inside the squares marked with that number. At first, scores stayed stubbornly at chance.

Then Cox asked them to make the dice show the same number as the squares. That is, if the person chose five, he would try to make the dice not only fall into the squares marked five, but stop with five showing on the top of each die. Scores immediately went up. Some people showed a modest amount of PK.

Over the years, laboratory tests with dice showed the same effects as ESP experiments had. Talented people made strong scores in the beginning, then seemed to lose their powers. If feedback helped PK, there was little sign of it here. Seeing the dice stop on the desired number gave people immediate feedback, yet their scores continued to decline.

Researchers have tried to show PK in other ways. Cox put a wooden pendulum into a box. The pendulum was driven by an electric motor and connected to a counter. When it swung wide, an electric switch advanced the counter. The farther the pendulum swung, the farther the counter advanced. People tried to make the pendulum either swing farther than the motor normally took it, or shorten the normal swing so that the counter did not advance at all. Their scores were enough above chance for Cox to conclude that PK can affect the swing of the pendulum.

In 1928, forty years before Cox hunted for PK with a pendulum, a woman in Denmark was using her mind to move pendulums. Anna Rasmussen had also shown other strong signs of PK and convinced researchers of her talent. Then in 1956, Anna was tested again. A pendulum was placed inside a glass box. She stood several feet from the box and tried to make the pendulum swing so wide that it would strike the glass wall. This time Anna was plainly successful with her own pendulum, but didn't do very well with those brought in by other experimenters. No trickery was found, but this kind of result makes it impossible to declare that Anna's PK was genuine.

Other parapsychologists have brought atomic physics into the search for PK. Not even a physicist can predict when a decaying element will throw off its next particle, so John Beloff and L. Evans decided to use the natural process of radioactivity decay in a PK experiment that would allow no one to cheat. They set up a counter that would register each time a decaying particle struck it and asked people to try to change the rate of decay. The person being tested first spent a minute trying to speed up the counter, then another minute trying to slow it down. Thirty students tried their hand, but the experiment turned up no evidence of PK.

Helmut Schmidt, who used strontium 90 to test for precognition, found that some of his subjects could influence radioactive decay. His machine showed a circle of nine small lights that lit up, one at a time. The switch that controlled the lights had two positions; whenever a radioactive particle struck it, it turned on the next light in the circle. During the experiment, the switch moved rapidly back and forth between the two positions. If it was struck while in position one, the next light in a clockwise direction went on. If it was struck while in position two, the next light in a counterclockwise direction turned on. The person being tested tried to make the lights move around the circle in the same direction.

In the course of the experiment, Schmidt turned up a *psi-misser*. Parapsychologists say that people who score consistently below chance are showing psi-missing, which they believe indicates psychic ability. Some people deliberately miss. Others are so uncomfortable at the thought of possessing ESP or PK that they unconsciously push away their ability in what amounts to psychic sabotage.

Schmidt's psi-misser was another parapsychologist who moved the lights counterclockwise no matter how hard he tried to light them in the other direction. Schmidt's other prize subject was a girl who could move the lights in the desired direction.

Looked at separately, their signs of PK are not impressive. Each tried to influence the lights 6400 times. Purely by chance, each should have succeeded 3200 times. The psi-misser's score was less than 160 below chance; the girl's score was no more than 160 above. The laws of probability tell us that the two scores, added together, beat the odds by more than ten million to one, but such a display of PK is not likely to open closed doors or move objects through the air. And parapsychologists would also admit that if we disregard psi-missing and average the two scores, they would wipe each other out. We'd be right back at chance.

In the USSR lives a woman who seems to have a talent for PK and even controls it. Nina Kulagina's ability came to light when she told her physician that she seemed to be clairvoyant. When embroidering, she always, without looking, pulled the right color thread from a bag.

Her doctor took her to Leonid Vasiliev, a Soviet scientist, who began by investigating her clairvoyance but wound up studying PK. He gave Kulagina a compass and asked her to move the needle. She concentrated and the needle immediately swung away from the north.

Such an uncontrolled experiment is no proof of PK, but Kulagina has been tested repeatedly by Russian researchers for many years. Genady Sergeev, a neurophysiologist, said that by 1970 Kulagina had passed more than one hundred tests.

For a long time, the only evidence of her talents seen in the West was a series of films made in the Soviet Union. The movies, which were smuggled into England, showed Kulagina swinging compass needles and making matchboxes, salt shakers, matches, and cigarettes move across a table. Although the movies showed no evidence of trickery, parapsychologists knew that it is possible to fool the camera.

At last American and English parapsychologists got a chance to see Kulagina at work. On several occasions they watched her use PK and recorded the display on film. None of them tested her under strict conditions, so they cannot say that her ability has been proved. But most believe that she could pass a laboratory test.

Sergeev reports that when Kulagina makes objects move her heart races, her blood pressure rises, she breathes rapidly, and strong brain waves can be recorded from the back of her head. After a half-hour's work, she is two pounds lighter, her head aches, she feels dizzy and often vomits.

J. Gaither Pratt, who has visited Kulagina three times, points out that she works on objects that visitors bring in, objects that she has no chance to attach to wires or threads. The visitors also take their test objects away with them and can try different ways of reproducing Kulagina's feats by trickery.

Once Pratt spread red aquarium gravel over a table. Kulagina moved a small metal cylinder through the gravel, leaving a trail. On another occasion she tried to move a plastic jelly container that Pratt had brought from the airplane. She strained and strained, but the plastic dish did not move. Suddenly, a small block of wood on the other side of the container — and four inches farther from Kulagina than the jelly dish — began to rotate toward her.

When Pratt visited her with Australian parapsychologist Jurgen Keil, Kulagina moved a Ping-Pong ball, which was attached by a spring to the inside of an open plastic cube. As she concentrated, the ball moved against the pull of the spring, pressing down against the floor of the cube. As Pratt says, none of these displays proves anything, but even with the help of strings and magnets, the parapsychologists could not duplicate Kulagina's feats with the Ping-Pong ball.

9

Cow's Blood and Cotton

If thoughts can move a plastic cube through a pile of gravel or overcome the pull of the magnetic pole, perhaps they can also affect living tissue. Many believe they can.

In Baltimore, Maryland, Olga Worrall has been healing the sick for many years. Olga uses no penicillin, no aspirin, no scalpels, or sutures; her only tool is her mind. She works her cure in churches, first spending an hour in prayers and explanations, then laying her hands upon the sick.

One woman who had an ugly red growth on her cheek said she found the tumor melting away after Olga touched it. But in most cases, her touch does not knit broken bones, transform withered limbs, or straighten deformed spines. Her patients improve gradually. Sometimes they don't get well, but so many do that doctors often send her people they cannot help.

Olga believes that her ability to heal is God's gift, but she does not call herself a faith healer or a miracle worker. She regards the healing as no more miraculous than the growth of a flower or the patter of rain. Olga is unusual among healers because she insists that her patients see a doctor and because she refuses to accept money.

Until her husband, Ambrose, died in 1972, the Worralls worked as a team. Their first patient was a four-year-old boy. The little boy's eyes were badly crossed and rolled wildly when he tried to focus them. He would never be able to read or write, said doctors, until he had surgery.

Olga laid her hands on the boy's head and thought of Christ healing the child. Within three months, the boy's eyes were normal. Within four years, he threw away his glasses.

Ambrose once healed a nine-year-old girl who was suffering from von Recklinghausen's disease, an affliction that is usually fatal. Laboratory tests had shown the presence of the disease. After three weeks of daily treatments, the girl was visibly better. Her symptoms gradually disappeared, and four years later she was still healthy.

None of Ambrose's or Olga's cures can be proved to the satisfaction of scientists. There is no way to show that it was the laying on of hands and not the natural processes of people's bodies that healed them. But neither is there any way to prove that the Worralls' psychokinetic powers did not restore their health.

Many people say that they have the power to make the lame walk, the blind see, and the cancer victim whole. In the United States, most of them claim that they are only a channel for the power of God. A twist of the TV dial on any Sunday morning will bring at least one of these healers into your living room.

Parapsychologists believe that this kind of healing, if it exists, is a clear case of PK. Most doctors and psychologists believe that such cures can be explained without resorting to PK.

Until recently, Kathryn Kuhlman was the best known of these religious healers. She said that she never healed anyone, that the Holy Spirit worked the cures through her. When she came to a city, thousands flocked to the auditorium. After a choir sang hymns and the audience filled baskets with cash and checks, Kuhlman began to preach.

Suddenly, she broke off her sermon and announced that the Holy Spirit was healing a member of the audience. Someone stood up, claimed he had been cured, and miracles seemed to happen. At a single service, hundreds of people said that their cancers disappeared, cataracts slipped from their eyes, and deformed joints straightened.

Parapsychologist Ian Stevenson investigated six people who claimed that they had been cured by Kathryn Kuhlman. Not one of them had a verified physical disease that could be shown to have disappeared.

William A. Nolen, a surgeon, acted as an usher at Kuhlman's service in Minneapolis. More than a hundred people in the crowd of ten thousand came forward and described the diseases the dynamic preacher had cured: asthma, bursitis, arthritis, backaches, cancer, multiple sclerosis, and paralysis.

Nolen got as many names and addresses as he could and

two months later contacted twenty-three of the people who said they had been cured. One had already died of cancer; a second died within another two months. Some people still claimed that they had been cured, but none of them had any evidence, such as x-rays or laboratory tests made before and after the healing, to show that a disease had ever existed and that it no longer was present. A number of them still showed symptoms of the disease they insisted Kuhlman had healed.

On the other hand, J. Gaither Pratt and Naomi Hintze found one girl whose bone cancer disappeared after she attended one of Kuhlman's services. Lisa Larios' cancer had been discovered by x-rays and verified by surgery. Her doctors said that chemotherapy and radiation might give her six months of life, but that the outlook was very serious. During the service, Lisa felt a great warmth in her body. She began to improve rapidly and her symptoms disappeared. X-rays, taken a year later, showed no signs of cancer.

There is one factor that makes it impossible to attribute the healing solely to Kathryn Kuhlman's power. For ten days Lisa had had chemotherapy. Pratt points out that the cure may have been the result of the therapy and that Lisa's visit to the Shrine Auditorium just happened to take place at the time her cancer had begun to heal. We'll never know.

Kathryn Kuhlman is no longer healing the sick. She died in 1976 after having open-heart surgery.

Over a hundred years ago, a fourteen-year-old girl, Bernadette Soubirous, saw a vision of the Virgin near a grotto at Lourdes, France. The Virgin instructed Bernadette to dig in the ground. Where she dug, a stream sprang forth. Its waters are said to cure the sick. Each year, two million crippled and dying people journey to Lourdes to bathe in its healing waters.

Although the grotto is lined with the canes and crutches of the cured, the Roman Catholic Church claims few miracles. Between 1935 and 1950, only eleven cases met the standards the Church declared necessary for a cure. D. J. West, a British psychiatrist, investigated all eleven cases. None, he said, could be considered a miracle. Either there was no medical evidence that a disease existed before the visit, or the cure could be explained by other means.

Within the past few years, strange stories have come from Brazil and the Philippines. Healers in both countries were performing psychic surgery. They removed tumors, gallstones, and other diseased organs without using knives or scalpels. The patient's skin appeared to part and blood flowed, but there was no pain, no incision, and no stitches. The patient walked away from the operating table, apparently healed.

Psychic surgery became so popular that travel agents arranged tours to the Philippines for people who needed medical aid. Over two thousand people went on these healing tours.

In 1972, the first films of psychic surgeon Tony Agpaoa were shown in this country. Parapsychologist Stanley Krippner said that the substances Agpaoa pulled from his patients' bodies looked suspiciously like chicken entrails, and he detected signs of trickery. A second film, shown the next year, was also an obvious fake.

Then Krippner met a California businessman who swore

that in ten minutes Agpaoa had removed a tumor from his brain. The healer had promised to give the businessman the tumor, but later said he had lost it. A film of the operation showed Agpaoa kneading the man's forehead, a red fluid gushing out, and a white mass appearing in Agpaoa's hand.

Krippner decided to visit the Philippines and watch psychic surgeons at work. He went from place to place and observed a number of them. Nemesio Taylo, who was operating on a young man with stomach pains, apparently pulled four thick strips of white cloth from the patient's abdomen. The same surgeon pulled a strip of plastic from the navel of a woman with backaches. From a boy's abdomen, he pulled a clay-covered band of elastic. Several times Krippner watched slits appear in the skin and blood, pus, or a waxlike fluid ooze out. At no time did he detect trickery.

Finally, Krippner submitted to psychic surgery himself. The surgeon, Josephine Sison, touched his abdomen and red liquid began to trickle down his flanks. Then she pressed an oil-soaked wad of cotton to one side of his abdomen. The cotton disappeared and she pulled it out, through the skin, from the other side. It was now streaked with red. Again, Krippner could find no fraud.

But when William Nolen visited the Philippines, he found nothing but fraud. He saw surgeons swab abdomens with cotton, at the same time scratching the skin with a sharp piece of mica they had hidden in their palms. When they waved their bare hands above the patients' bodies, blood appeared as if by magic. The cuts were like those sometimes made by the edge of paper. At first the skin looks smooth, then blood begins to ooze through the slit.

Nolen was shown what he was told were blood clots, appendixes, and other diseased organs as surgeons removed them from abdomens and cast them into pails. Instead, he saw pieces of blood-soaked cotton, the organs of small animals, and chunks of yellow fat soaked in a red liquid. He watched a surgeon seem to pull an eye partway out of a socket, wipe it off, and allow it to return to its place. Then he observed the surgeon quickly place the eye of a cat or dog, which he had palmed before the operation, onto a shelf out of the audience's view.

Like Krippner, Nolen allowed a psychic surgeon to operate upon him. As the operation began, Nolen tensed his abdominal muscles. Although the surgeon's fingers appeared to pass into his abdomen, Nolen could tell by the pressure against the muscles that the fingers remained outside the skin.

Despite Nolen's report, Krippner still believes that psychic surgery sometimes is genuine. But travel agents no longer send Americans to the Philippines on psychic surgery tours. In 1974, the Federal Trade Commission stopped the practice.

After the tours were stopped, a hearing was held in Seattle. The testimony piled up. Carol and Donald Wright said that they had believed in the power of psychic surgery — until they studied with Filipino surgeons. Then they discovered that the surgeons palmed pieces of animal tissue, stones, and strings that they pretended to remove from patients' bodies, and what they called *bullets* — wads of cotton that held clots of cow's blood. Donald Wright showed the court how he could perform psychic surgery on a bath towel. The towel bled; spectators saw what appeared to be open flesh; Wright removed pieces of animal tissue and closed the incision.

A professional magician told of catching a psychic surgeon slicing a patient's skin with a razor blade hidden in cotton, just as Nolen had seen a sharp piece of mica being used. Doctors told about cancer patients who had visited the Filipino surgeons, and then died because their cancers had gone untreated. The judge listened to the testimony and, on February 27, 1975, ruled that "psychic surgery is pure and unmitigated fakery."

10

Mice, Rye, and Barley

From the evidence, it appears that psychic surgery is trickery. But psychic surgeons cure some people as thoroughly as doctors do. So did Kathryn Kuhlman and so do Olga Worrall and other healers. No doctor and no psychologist would deny this.

The human body generally heals itself. In most cases, the job of the doctor is to get the healing process started. In some people, it begins as soon as an injury or illness attacks the body. In others, it starts slowly.

No one knows just why or how the healing starts. But we know that if a patient believes the doctor — or the healer — has the power to cure him, chances are that he will begin to get well. If a doctor gives pills made of simple sugar to one hundred people suffering from headaches, toothaches, backaches, or other pain, thirty-six of them will stop hurting.

Researchers call these sugar pills *placebos* and this response to a fake medicine, the *placebo effect*. When drug companies test a new antibiotic, they have to arrange what are called *double-blind* tests to avoid the placebo effect. If either the patients or the doctors know which pills are antibiotics and which are placebos, any new drug will seem to work miracles. But when no one knows who is getting the real medicine, the effect of the drug on the body becomes plain.

The human mind and body are closely linked. Worry, fear, sorrow, lust, or joy can affect the heart, lungs, blood vessels, intestines, bladder, and even the eyes. When we get upset or tense, nervous or afraid, secretions pour into our bloodstream and change the way our bodies work. Doctors say we are stressed. If the stress lasts for weeks or months, we may become ill.

The list of diseases that can come from stress is long. It includes asthma, colitis, constipation, diarrhea, ulcers, upset stomachs, migraine headaches, high blood pressure, rashes, allergies, and loss of hair. Some doctors believe that stress plays a part in most disease, even infectious ones like tuberculosis or influenza. A person under stress is unable to fight off invading bacteria and viruses.

Doctors sometimes cure patients suffering from stress-induced diseases by persuading them to relax. They talk to them for hours; they give them placebos. When it works, the cure comes from suggestion. Psychic healers can cure in the same way. Neither the doctor nor the psychic healer does anything to the patient's body. He simply puts the patient into a condition so that the body can heal itself.

Many diseases disappear by themselves, no matter what doctors or healers do. Such ailments are called *self-limiting* diseases, and treatment can only make the patient feel better while the disease runs its course. But if the person has seen a psychic healer, the healer gets credit for the cure — just as the doctor gets the credit when his patient gets well.

Some people get well when doctors think they shouldn't. William Nolen once had a patient with a cancer that had spread throughout his body. The cancer slowly shrank, the man's symptoms went away, and, when Nolen later removed the man's appendix, he could find no sign of the cancer. When a disease disappears in this way, doctors call it *spontaneous regression*. It happens rarely; Nolen has seen it only once among 1400 cancer patients. Doctors think that spontaneous regression takes place about once in every ten thousand cases.

Some psychic cures could be cases of spontaneous regression. It is also possible that cases of spontaneous regression could be examples of psychic healing.

Radiologist O. Carl Simonton and psychologist Stephanie Simonton believe that some cancer patients can cure themselves. They treat all their patients with radiation, but they also use PK. The Simontons call it *visualization therapy*. They ask their patients to imagine the cancer within their bodies and the white blood cells that fight against it. The Simontons say that most people who can see their bodies winning and watch the cancer slowly shrinking, recover; those who imagine the disease defeating the white cells don't.

Perhaps psychic healers do more than merely suggest to patients that they will get well. Many of the cures that do not meet scientific standards may, nevertheless, be the result of PK. Critics have never shown that PK did *not* cure some of the cases they have investigated. They have simply said that there was not enough evidence to prove that the cure came from PK.

Healers may use PK to push a patient's own healing system into action. Studies of Oskar Estebany, a Hungarian healer, suggest that they may. At McGill University in Canada, physiologist Bernard Grad tested Estebany's powers. Using scissors, Grad cut pieces of skin, about a half-inch wide, from the backs of mice. After the wounds were traced on a piece of clear plastic as a record, Grad divided the animals into three groups.

Each group was placed in a small container. Estebany held one container between his hands for half an hour each day. A person with no healing ability held the second container in the same way. The third group of mice was not treated. The wounds on Estebany's mice did not vanish overnight, but the mice he held did heal much faster than any of the other mice. Estebany's touch seemed to speed the animals' natural healing processes.

Estebany's power appears to extend to plants. Grad planted barley seeds in three different containers. The first group was watered with water from a bottle that Estebany had held between his hands. The second group was watered from a bottle held by another person, the third with untreated water. More of the seeds watered from the bottle held by Estebany sprouted, and the barley plants grew larger than those from the other seeds.

Ten years after Grad worked with Estebany, Sister Justa Smith, a Franciscan nun who is a biochemist, studied the healer again. This time she asked him to hold a flask filled with an enzyme solution. The enzyme was trypsin, which plays a role in the body's natural healing process. A magnetic field speeds up the activity of trypsin; ultraviolet light damages the enzyme and slows it down.

When Estebany held a flask of trypsin for seventy-five minutes, the enzyme speeded up, just as did the solution in a second flask that was exposed to a strong magnetic field. When Estebany held a flask filled with trypsin that had been damaged by ultraviolet light, the solution acted like normal trypsin.

Then one of the troubles that plague parapsychology descended. When the experiment was repeated under the direction of Sister Justa Smith's lab assistant, Estebany had almost no effect on the enzymes.

In one test, Estebany appeared to affect the bodies of nineteen people. Dolores Krieger arranged an experiment in which Estebany treated each person once or twice a day. The patients, who were taken off all medication during the test, looked and felt better. Krieger drew blood from each patient before and after the six-day treatment. The hemoglobin content of the patients' blood had increased after the treatment. Nine other patients, who lived under the same conditions as the experimental patients, showed no change in hemoglobin levels.

Once again, such experiments are interesting but prove nothing. All nineteen patients were eager to be treated by Estebany. The nine other patients knew they were not treated by Estebany. The experiment was not a double-blind, therefore the results could be simply the result of the placebo effect.

Krieger repeated her experiment twice, and each time the patients who were treated by Estebany showed an increase in hemoglobin. But Estebany's hemoglobin level did not change, nor did the temperature of his hands alter. Krieger believes that Estebany's touch starts a person's own healing process to work.

Estebany's influence on barley seeds apparently was no fluke. Olga and Ambrose Worrall were asked to influence the growth of rye grass by "holding the seedlings in their thoughts." The rye plants were growing at .00625 inch per hour. At 9 P.M., when the Worralls began to think of the plants, growth slowly speeded up. By eight o'clock the next morning, the rye was growing at .0525 inch per hour. During the night, the rye should have grown one-sixteenth inch; instead, it grew more than half an inch. The amazing part of this experiment is that the Worralls stayed in their home, over six hundred miles away from the grass in Robert Miller's laboratory.

In other experiments, Olga Worrall has influenced the particles in an atomic cloud chamber; healers in Iceland have speeded up the growth of yeast; and in North Carolina, some people have used their thoughts to rouse mice from anesthesia. Psychic healing appears to have some basis. Although the evidence is still slight, it exists.

But the evidence is not strong enough to bet one's life on it. Patients with cancer or pneumonia who go to psychic healers instead of to doctors could be going to their deaths. Sometimes early medical treatment can cure a disease that, treated later or not at all, is fatal. Many people have postponed cancer surgery, hoping that psychic healers could cure their tumors. Most of those people are now dead.

William Nolen checked several people who supposedly had been cured by Filipino psychic surgeons. The man who had introduced him to the surgeons was enthusiastic about their powers. He believed they had cured a brain tumor in his four-year-old daughter. Two years after psychic surgeons spent eight weeks treating the child, she died.

Another man with bowel trouble chose psychic surgeons instead of an operation in an American hospital. He believed he was cured. For nearly a year, he had no serious trouble, just "a little soreness." Then, about nine months after his psychic surgery, his intestines perforated and doctors had to make an emergency opening for his bowel. His case could once have been cured with a single operation. Now he faces two more serious operations.

A woman who developed lung cancer visited the Philippines instead of having the operation her doctor recommended. She swore she was healed, until the night several months later when she began to cough up blood. Doctors opened her chest and found the cancer had spread. She died of it.

As long as patients see both doctors and healers, as Olga Worrall insists they do, it will be impossible to prove that PK can heal. But more people will be alive who think that it does.

PART FOUR

Curiosities

"Curiouser and curiouser!" cried Alice (she was so much surprised, that for a moment she quite forgot how to speak good English).

Lewis Carroll,
Alice's Adventures in Wonderland

11

Glowing Fingers and Telepathic Plants

Although psychic surgery has been thoroughly discredited, some parapsychologists refuse to admit that it is a fraud. Others have their own favorite corners of ESP or PK that seem unlikely to tell us much about the paranormal.

Around 1970, some were bewitched by a process called Kirlian photography. Word came that Russian scientists had succeeded in photographing a halo that surrounded all living matter. Leaves, fingertips, and flowers seemed to generate a glowing field. The pictures were made by laying a leaf or pressing a fingertip on a piece of film and then passing electricity through the back of the film.

Parapsychologist Thelma Moss went to the Soviet Union, where she was neither permitted to meet Valentina and Semyon Kirlian, who had developed the process, nor to visit the laboratory where the pictures were taken. The

Russian researchers insisted that Kirlian photographs could show the presence of disease, and they displayed a picture of a phantom leaf. For this photography, a piece was cut out of a leaf before it was laid on the film. The developed picture showed a whole leaf, with the severed section glowing like a faint ghost beside the brighter portion that remained.

The next year, Kendall Johnson, one of Moss's students at UCLA, was impressed by the Russian slides of glowing leaves and radiant fingers. Johnson read one of the Russian research papers and managed to take his own Kirlian pictures.

Before long, both Moss and Johnson were turning out a flood of photographs. Moss studied the subject at UCLA, and other parapsychologists at Sonoma State College in California and at Newark, New Jersey, began to work at it.

For years, psychics had claimed to see halos around human bodies, flickering like flames that varied in color and size. They called them *auras,* and said that saints generated a blue-violet aura, which indicated their religious feeling. Various shades of gray, green, red, brown, orange, or yellow indicated selfishness, fear, jealousy, anger, love, greed, pride, or intelligence.

Some believed the psychics had been vindicated. A few enthusiastic parapsychologists began to talk about "bioenergy" and suggested that each plant, animal, or person has a "bioplasmic body" that surrounds it, a body made of energy.

The only hitch was that the halo was not limited to living matter. Rocks, coins, paper, magnets, can openers, liquids, all glowed obediently for the photographs. But researchers were not discouraged. The halo around living things changed, while that given off by inert objects was constant.

By 1972, when parapsychologist D. Scott Rogo visited one of the three labs where most of the research took place, Kirlian photography had become the latest fad. But Rogo soon discovered that the researchers knew little about the process. Twice he secretly licked his finger before pressing it on the film, and no halo appeared in the photographs. The young researcher said that this had "great psychic significance."

Then, Rogo reports, he showed the young man that body heat could affect the aura and that he could change its size by pressing harder on the film. Although he showed the researcher how to install a cheap weighing device so that pressure could not alter the photographs, it was not done. Another Kirlian researcher told Rogo that such controlled experiments weren't necessary.

What many Kirlian enthusiasts prefer to forget, says Rogo, is that for many years industrial plants used a similar process to find defects in metals. Electricity causes the discharge of ions and electrons, which show up on a piece of film.

Two researchers believe that the Kirlian effect is simply this "corona discharge." William Tiller, a Stanford University expert on metals, likens the Kirlian effect to lightning or to St. Elmo's fire, the glowing ball of light that sailors often see hovering around a ship's mast during a storm at sea. Pilots are well acquainted with St. Elmo's fire, which is an electrical discharge. When they fly their planes through dry snow, ice crystals, or near a thunderstorm, the glow often surrounds the aircraft's nose, windshield, or wing tips.

William Joines, at Duke University, agrees. He produced a picture that did even better than the Kirlians' phantom leaf. He showed off a picture of a phantom rock.

Another team of researchers believes that the aura is simply a measure of water in the skin — the drier the skin, the brighter and larger the aura. Physicists John O. Pehek and David L. Faust and psychologist Harry J. Kyler studied Kirlian photography for the Defense Department. They found that a finger dunked in alcohol, which removes water from the skin, produced impressive Kirlian streamers, whereas a finger soaked in water produced almost nothing, (Rogo had eliminated his own Kirlian aura by sucking his finger before he laid it on the film.)

Wood, they said, worked the same way. Dry wood produced spectacular auras; wet wood showed nothing.

This team of researchers believes that moisture in the fingers affects the electric discharge that is passed through the film. The wetter the finger, the smaller the discharge, and the smaller the discharge, the dimmer the aura. Pehek, Faust, and Kyler say that the aura's color depends on body chemistry, such as changes in the amount of salt in a person's sweat.

The Kirlian aura is a normal, not a paranormal, effect. Differences in auras can come from many things: body chemistry, emotion, sweat, pressure, heat, the twitch of a finger on the film, a drink or two of whiskey, and a multitude of other natural causes. Any can change the size and color of the radiance. It appears to be of no help in the search for evidence of ESP.

Another incident that most parapsychologists would like to forget involved telepathic plants. In 1968, Cleve Backster reported that plants could sense the intentions of human beings. If a person approached a flower or a carrot, intending to jerk it from the ground, the threatened plant reacted in fear. What is more, nearby plants also reacted to this murder of their own kind.

Backster, a lie-detector expert, said he got this information by hooking electrodes to a plant's leaf and connecting the plant to a lie detector. When a plant was threatened with destruction or "saw" other plants perish, the detector recorded a jump, the same reaction that people show under strong emotion.

Excitement over telepathic plants was still high when Backster reported that shrimp were as good as daisies at emotional reaction. When he boiled shrimp in the presence of their fellows, the watching shrimp set the lie detector jiggling.

A number of researchers tried to get the same kind of results. Shrimp were boiled, salt was poured on slugs, and flats of flowers threatened or uprooted. But the "watching" shrimp, slugs, and plants did not react. Then Rex Johnson, a researcher at the University of Washington, showed that Backster's results came from changes in temperature and humidity. When both temperature and humidity were controlled, the lie detector never wavered, no matter how much Johnson mistreated plants or animals.

But when the atmosphere in the room fluctuated normally, the recording pen jumped as a draft blew through the room, or people moved around, or boiling shrimp sent clouds of steam swirling about the room.

Later reports that others had detected electrical signals from dishes of yogurt and lime jello helped to turn parapsychological interest abruptly away from such unpromising lines of research.

12

Clever Hans

Early in this century, all Germany was talking about a horse. Not because it was beautiful or because it could run faster than other horses, but because it was so intelligent. Clever Hans belonged to a German math teacher named Wilhelm van Osten. The horse worked arithmetic problems almost as well as his master. He could spell, read, and figure out simple tunes.

Sometimes Hans told people his answers by tapping with his hoof. If someone said, "How much is three times five?" he would tap fifteen times, then stop. If asked which playing card his master was holding, Hans would stomp his foot once for an ace, twice for a king, three times for a queen, and so on. He could also answer questions by nodding his head for "yes" and shaking it from side to side for "no." Van Osten constructed an alphabet chart and Hans would spell out words by tapping their place on the chart, stomping his foot first for the row and then for the letter's position in the row.

No one could figure out how a horse could be so intelligent. Two groups of scientists, many of them experts on the ways of animals, came to see Hans. The horse answered all their questions. The scientists kept a sharp eye on both the horse and his master, but van Osten never said a word that would let the horse know when to start tapping and when to stop. Neither group could find any trickery. Hans was apparently a genius.

But a German psychologist was not convinced. Oskar Pfungst conducted a series of experiments with Hans and his master. He found that the horse could answer a question only when the person who asked it knew the answer. Was Hans reading the questioner's mind? Pfungst soon found that he was not; this was not a case of ESP. The questioner had to stand within view of the horse.

Once he learned this, Pfungst watched the questioners closely. He discovered that, after asking Hans a question, a person always bent his head toward the horse, expecting the animal to answer. The movement was so slight that most people did not notice it, but the tiny inclination of the head was Hans's cue to start tapping.

When the horse's taps answered the question, the questioner showed that he was satisfied with the answer. He either pulled back his head or raised an eyebrow. Hans, being a clever horse, had learned that this was a signal to stop.

Pfungst also found that if the person who asked the question stood stiff and did not lean over to watch the horse,

Hans did not answer at all. And the psychologist discovered that he could get any answer he wanted from the horse by bending over and then straightening up. He didn't even have to ask the question.

For example, if someone asked Hans to add two and three, the questioner might lean forward expectantly until Hans had tapped five times, straighten up, signaling the horse to stop. Pfungst merely leaned forward, then straightened up after Hans had tapped five times.

Questioners gave the same kind of unintentional cues when they asked Hans to spell. Those tiny signals of head, or hand, or eyebrow, always came along to tell the animal when he had tapped enough times, first for the letter's row, then for its position on the chart.

Hans had picked up the same sort of cues that critics of parapsychology claim spoil many ESP experiments, cues that tell the subject what the researcher wants him to say or do.

Almost twenty years later, the story of Clever Hans seemed to repeat itself. This time the animal was Lady Wonder, a black horse that lived in Richmond, Virginia. According to J. B. Rhine, Lady was a restless, poorly trained, four-year-old filly.

Talking to Lady was much quicker than talking to Hans. Instead of using her hoof to tap out an answer, she touched her nose to blocks. In front of the horse were spread wooden blocks, and on each block was painted a letter or number. Lady could answer any question or work any arithmetical problem — as long as someone in the room knew the answer and wrote it down on a tablet.

The horse had always been close to human beings.

When she was only two months old, her mother died, and she was raised by her owners, who fed her from a baby bottle. Each time they went to the pasture to call her, Lady seemed to know she was wanted and came running from the far end of the field before she was called. Her owners decided that the horse could read their minds, made the set of blocks, and trained her to use them.

Word spread about Lady's telepathic powers and the Rhines came to see her. Lady's owner was always part of the show. She talked during Lady's demonstrations, moved around the barn, and tapped the stall with a riding crop. The Rhines suspected that she was watching the movements of the pencil as people wrote down the answers, and then signaling to the horse.

Rhine asked Lady to tell him the date on a coin he held in his hand. When he wrote the answer, he used a stubby pencil, one so short the owner could not watch the moving end. He waited. Lady lowered her head and, one by one, nudged the correct blocks.

Asking the horse a series of questions, Rhine gradually moved the owner farther and farther from the animal. Lady still gave the right answer. Then Rhine put up a piece of cardboard so that Lady could not see her owner. He even stopped writing down the answers. Lady was still right, six out of ten times.

Rhine reported that he could find no codes and no frauds. He couldn't be sure, he said, but it looked to him as if the horse might be reading people's minds. More tests were needed.

The Rhines went back to Richmond and ran more experiments. This time it was the story of Clever Hans all over again. When Lady could not see her owner, she could not answer a question. The Rhines also detected the signals that the owner was passing to her horse, signals like those that made Hans seem so clever.

The discovery did not end Lady's career. Until the horse died at the age of thirty-one, she kept convincing people that she was reading their minds. Her owner built her a special typewriter with large, soft rubber keys so that she could type her answers instead of nudging blocks. It was said that Lady could even predict the future — from horse races to presidential elections. But no parapsychologist ever tested her again.

Rhine still can't explain why the horse did so well on his early visits. He suspects that Lady may at times have been telepathic, but he has no proof. Lady may never have read minds. She may have been another clever horse. Her stunts as a young filly are not surprising. Even wild birds show up regularly to be fed, and a breeze blowing across a pasture would carry the scent of her owners long before they got close enough to call. If animal psi had to depend on Hans and Lady, the story would end here.

It was nearly fifty years before parapsychologists believed they had found another animal psychic. This time the animal was a dog named Chris, a part-beagle mongrel that belonged to Mr. and Mrs. George Wood of Greenwich, Rhode Island. Like Clever Hans, Chris answered questions with his paw. He could do simple mathematics and he could spell, for he replied, letter by letter, pawing at his owner's sleeve. It was said that Chris could even predict horse races.

Chris entertained the Woods' friends, performed at parties, and even appeared on TV. As he became famous, word reached Rhine's laboratory at Duke University, and researchers came to see the dog. They watched with interest as he answered questions and decided to check the animal for ESP.

In the first experiment, R. J. Cadoret prepared packs of Zener cards to test Chris for clairvoyance. Cadoret shuffled the cards and sealed them in black envelopes. The dog's master conducted the experiment and, using the numbers from one to five to represent the symbols on the cards, Chris pawed out the order of the deck. Twenty times Chris went through packs of Zener cards. Whether Wood was alone with the dog or in the company of others, the animal consistently showed remarkable signs of clairvoyance.

Then Cadoret tested Chris. The dog's scores immediately dropped.

J. Gaither Pratt took over and set up a test for telepathy. He shuffled the packs of cards, wrote down the order of the deck, and sealed each pack in a box. Wood sat in one room and a friend sat in another.

Sometimes Wood opened the box, took out the deck, cut it — but did not shuffle it — and went through the cards. As he looked at a card, he tried to send the symbol to Chris, who sat in the other room with Wood's friend. Chris pawed out the answers and the friend recorded them.

At other times, the friend opened the box and sent the symbols, while Chris sat in the room with Wood and pawed out the answers. Either way, Chris' scores were high enough to convince Pratt that telepathy was involved.

No one knows just who was telepathic. Pratt says that

perhaps Wood was the psychic. Without knowing it, he may have given Chris cues with his body. That would explain why Chris lost his clairvoyance when Cadoret himself tested him. Chris becomes another Clever Hans.

Pratt, however, is not sure. If Chris picked up body cues, then the friend who helped in the telepathy experiment would also have to be telepathic. But perhaps no one was psychic. In that last experiment, no parapsychologist was around to make sure that Wood and his friend followed the rules closely. The only time a researcher was on the premises, Chris failed. Pratt is willing to vouch for the honesty of Wood and his friend and discounts any chance of trickery.

Either Chris was psychic, or Chris was a clever dog with psychic friends, or the unsupervised experiments were botched, or trickery was involved. The question will never be answered; Chris is dead.

Many people who would be quick to laugh at reports of paw-tapping animals nevertheless believe in the ability researchers call *psi-trailing*. Everyone has heard tales of abandoned or lost animals who have traveled miles to find their masters. Most of them make their way across town or to the next village, but sometimes they seem to accomplish the impossible.

According to a book by Charles Alexander published in 1926, Bobbie, a collie, was separated from his human family in Indiana during a cross-country vacation trip. The family continued their vacation and returned home to Oregon. Fourteen months later Bobbie showed up at his master's restaurant in Silverton, Oregon.

Between 1940 and 1960, researchers at Duke collected cases of psi-trailing. They rejected most of the cases they heard about because they could not be sure that the animal that had turned up was the animal that had been lost, or because there were no witnesses, or because the report was too vague to check. After they eliminated all the suspicious stories, they were left with fifty-four animals that managed to find their masters: twenty-eight dogs, twenty-two cats, and four birds.

The most spectacular case was that of Sugar, a Persian cat with a deformed hip joint. Sugar was afraid of cars. When her owners moved from California to Oklahoma, they planned to take the cat, but she jumped from the car as they pulled out of the driveway. Sugar ran away, and her owners left. More than a year later, a Persian cat jumped in the open window of an Oklahoma barn and landed on a woman's back. At first the woman, who was Sugar's owner, thought that she had found a cat that merely looked like Sugar. Then she examined the animal and found the same deformed hip joint. Sugar had traveled fifteen hundred miles.

Many pet owners would say that their cats or dogs are psychic. The animals seem to know when strangers are coming, when their owners are leaving, when the people around them are happy or sad, angry or afraid. But such awareness does not mean that pets are telepathic, clairvoyant, or precognitive. Nor does psi-trailing necessarily have anything to do with psi.

Human beings have five senses: sight, smell, hearing, touch, and taste. Animals have the same senses but they work in different ways. A walk along the seashore or down a busy street is a very different experience for a dog and for his human owner.

Although the dog does not see color, he hears sounds that no human ear can detect and smells odors that no human nose can scent. The smells and sounds of his black and white world carry information that people can never pick up. As the dog trots along the sidewalk, he continually sniffs, reading the pavement as if it were a newspaper with articles describing each person and animal that recently passed by.

Compared to dogs, people can hardly smell a thing. Dogs use their noses to detect bombs or drugs for the police. They can also find people. A dog can tell who owns a discarded piece of clothing simply by sniffing it. The only time a dog is fooled is when the article belongs to an identical twin.

And animals aren't limited to sight, smell, hearing, taste, and touch. Some snakes, for example, have infrared sensors. They can "see" the heat that radiates from warm bodies. An animal hidden in the grass is as exposed to such a snake as if it were jumping up and down on a platter, shrieking, "Look at me."

Bats and dolphins have a sense called *echolocation*. Echolocation works just like radar. The animal locates objects by bouncing sound waves off them. The sense is so powerful that blinded bats can use it to tell the difference between objects that differ in size by as little as an inch.

Other animals use a combination of senses to perform seemingly magical feats. After traveling thousands of miles in the world's oceans, salmon swim back to the same small stream in which they were born. Some biologists believe that they have a built-in compass, but don't know just how it works. Some think that salmon use the tiny electrical charges caused by ocean currents passing through the earth's magnetic field. Others believe that the fish can tell one patch of an ocean from another by sampling the water for its salt content, which varies from place to place. Still others suspect that the fish navigate by using the moon as a guide. Most of them agree that, once the fish nears the region where its home stream empties into the sea, smell leads it the rest of the way. Just as each person has a unique scent, so does each body of water. As a dog sniffs its way to a person, salmon sniff their way back to their birthplace.

Birds use many cues to guide them on their yearly migrations. Psychologist Stephen Emlen found that indigo buntings navigate by the stars. He raised some of the birds in a planetarium that showed the constellation Orion in the north sky. When they were released in the fall, the birds used Betelgeuse, Orion's brightest star, as the North Star and flew off in the wrong direction, traveling east instead of south.

So psi-trailing may be nothing more than an animal's normal use of its senses. Although, as far as we know, dogs and cats lack the talents of snakes, bats, salmon, or birds, they may have the ability to develop some of these talents. People can't echolocate. But some blind people have learned to move through the world as surely as bats. Deprived of one sense, they have developed another, and they use bounced-off sound to make their way safely around obstacles.

However, if we can explain the case of Bobbie by saying that the collie navigated by the stars until he reached his part of Oregon and then used his nose to find his master's restaurant, that still leaves the case of Sugar. The Persian cat didn't return home. She traveled to a place she had never been before. Until we can explain Sugar's journey, we can't completely dismiss psi-trailing.

13

Animals in the Lab

Parapsychologists are aware that normal animal behavior can be confused with psychic ability. In 1952, J. B. Rhine tried to set up a situation in which dogs could not use their usual senses. The experiment was meant to test dogs for their ability to detect land mines, which are often planted in the path of an advancing army.

Rhine used small wooden boxes to simulate the mines and buried them along a line in the sand of a California beach. Each box was placed four inches under the sand at the bottom of a shallow tidepool. The water in the pools was from six to twelve inches deep. A light rain often rippled the surface of the water so that human beings, at least, could not see the bottom. A strong wind blowing from the ocean probably carried away a good deal of whatever scent the boxes gave off.

Neither the dogs, two German shepherds, nor their handlers knew where the boxes were buried. Once the boxes were beneath the surface, Rhine raked the entire beach so that the disturbed sand would not give away the position of the mines.

The beach was marked off in five-yard sections and each section divided into one-yard lengths. The dogs had to find the box in each section. If the dogs could not detect the boxes by smell, by sight, or by some other normal sense, they should have found one-fifth of the boxes. Instead, they found between one-third and one-half of them. The odds against such success are a thousand million to one. Rhine believes that ESP was surely involved.

He is not certain, however, whether the ESP belonged to the handlers or to the dogs. Perhaps Rhine found clairvoyant German shepherds or clairvoyant dog handlers. A simpler explanation is that dogs possess keener senses than we give them credit for.

Another experiment left parapsychologists wondering whether they were testing animal or human PK. Helmut Schmidt connected a metal grille to a device that periodically ran an electric current through it. He put cockroaches on the grille, supposing that if the bugs possessed PK, they would use their power to shut off the switch that started the current, thereby reducing the number of shocks. To his surprise, the current ran through the grille much oftener than the machine was set to deliver shocks. Either the cockroaches like to be shocked and therefore used PK to increase their pleasure, or Schmidt, who detests the bugs, subconsciously used PK to increase the bugs' pain.

Most parapsychologists who have heard of the experiment believe that, if PK was involved, Schmidt was the psychic.

About the same time Rhine tested German shepherds in California, Karlis Osis and Esther Foster were working with cats in North Carolina. They built a long, covered corridor and placed obstacles in it to confuse the cats. At the end of the passageway, they set two dishes of food. Before a cat was dropped into the corridor, Osis and Foster chose one of the dishes as the target, then tried to will the cat to go to the dish. At first, they were quite successful. A good many more animals went to the dish the researchers concentrated on, and they believed they had discovered that cats were either telepathic or clairvoyant. But the cats soon came to prefer one dish to the other and the scores dropped. No matter how hard the researchers concentrated, most cats went to their favorite dish.

They tried again, this time testing for clairvoyance. They used a simple maze, an open, T-shaped box. When a cat is placed at the base of the T, it runs along the narrow corridor until it comes to the branching arms. Sometimes it will run down one arm, sometimes down another.

An assistant placed food in one arm of the T and set fans to blow away any scent that might tip off the cats. Neither Osis nor Foster knew which arm held the food, so the cats could not use telepathy to find it. When cats ran in the maze, they chose the arm with the food in it more than half the time. But again, most animals soon turned the same way when they were put in the maze, and the scores dropped.

It looked as if both experiments were failures except for one thing. If a cat didn't go to its favorite dish, the scores went up. When Osis and Foster looked just at the times the cats broke their usual patterns, they found that the animals were more likely to be going, in the first experiment, to the dish the experimenters were concentrating on and, in the second, down the arm of the maze that held food. They believed that these cases of *random behavior* might indicate animal ESP, but they could not be positive. Perhaps it was ESP on the part of the researchers, or perhaps the cats were picking up the smell of food despite all of Osis and Foster's precautions.

Meanwhile, other experiments were going on, and some of them were cruel. In 1967, Robert Morris tested animals for precognition. He watched nineteen rats move about on a floor that had been marked off in squares. He counted the squares each rat covered in two minutes, then either killed each rat or spared it, making his choice by a number arbitrarily assigned to the rat. Because frightened rats usually freeze, Morris thought that the rats that were slated to die would run about less than the rats that were to live. Among sixteen of the nineteen rats, the doomed animals did cover fewer squares than the others, but the difference wasn't great enough to excite parapsychologists.

Next, Morris tested goldfish for precognition. Frightened fish swim about frantically. Instead of killing the goldfish, Morris dipped the previously chosen fish out of the water, holding them aloft in a net. He supposed that precognitive fish would be anxious and swim rapidly about the tank. This time the results were better. The fish that had been chosen to gasp in the air did swim about more than the others.

But none of these experiments showed strong enough

signs of ESP to do any more than suggest that maybe some animals might be precognitive or telepathic or clairvoyant. An Englishman, Nigel Richmond, had tested paramecia, tiny one-celled animals so small that they are invisible to the naked eye. Looking through a microscope, Richmond divided the area he could see into four parts. Then he willed the animals to move into a particular part. He said that he was successful, but no one else has reported the same kind of success.

While Morris was frightening goldfish, two French researchers were following up on Osis and Foster's experiments. Pierre Duval and Evelyn Montredon used the idea of random behavior to test mice for ESP. They built a cage with a wire floor divided in half by a low barrier. Each half of the floor was connected to a live wire, and from time to time a weak electric current passed through one side. The mouse's job was to avoid shock by jumping into the safe side of the cage.

The surges of electricity were determined by machinery, photoelectric cells detected each mouse's jumps, and the results of the experiment were recorded on punched tape. By these precautions, Duval and Montredon hoped to eliminate any human influence on the mice. The results of their experiment showed no evidence of psi; the mice were shocked just about as often as not.

But when the researchers looked only at random behavior, they thought they had a strong case. They eliminated each time the animal jumped the barrier immediately after it was shocked, reasoning that this was purely mechanical behavior. The mouse stayed in one side of the cage until it was shocked, then jumped to the other side and waited until it was shocked again.

Next they eliminated what they called *static behavior*. In these cases, the mouse stayed on the same side of the cage no matter what happened. Duval and Montredon thought that static behavior indicated the mouse was too frightened or too tired to jump, or that it did not feel the shock.

This left them with cases of random behavior, the times the mice jumped to the other side of the cage although they had received no shock. If no ESP was involved, the mice should have been shocked after half of these random jumps. In 1612 such jumps, the mice saved themselves from shock 53 times more than they should have. The odds against their success were more than a thousand to one. Duval and Montredon were convinced that the mice had been either precognitive or clairvoyant at least 53 times.

In a later experiment, they tested another ten wild mice in the same machine. Out of 8314 random jumps, the mice avoided electric shock 258 times more than they should have. The odds against this score were a million to one.

At last, it seemed, parapsychology had the evidence its critics had demanded. ESP existed — at least among mice. Parapsychologists were jubilant and they gave Duval and Montredon the McDougall Award for the year's most notable contribution to parapsychology.

All that was needed was for other researchers to repeat the French experiments. American researchers at Rhine's North Carolina Institute soon reported that they, too, got similar results from similar experiments. It appeared that the jumps of the French mice had not been a fluke.

Then the roof fell in. In 1974 one of the American researchers, Walter J. Levy, was caught cheating. He had been setting the recording device on his machine so that the animals appeared to be making correct guesses when they were doing no such thing. Unfortunately, Levy had taken part in most of the experiments that supported the French research. Parapsychologists stopped rejoicing and threw out every experiment that Levy had touched. The work had to begin again.

Other laboratories began to report success, but no one has turned up with the million to one scores obtained by Duval and Montredon. The best results have come from New York. Susan Harris and James Terry used rewards instead of punishment to test rats for precognition.

The same learning theory that tells us that feedback is usually necessary for learning also tells us that rewards often work better than electric shock. In this case, Harris and Terry chose water as the reward. If the rat wanted a drink, it had to press a bar to get it. But there were two bars in the cage. Sometimes one bar would release the water, sometimes the other. The thirsty rat had to guess which bar to press. When the researchers looked only at random behavior, the rat was getting more water than it should have. The odds against its success were five thousand to one.

In similar experiments, gerbils in Scotland showed signs of precognition when they had to press the right key to get sunflower seeds. But when other researchers at the University of Edinburgh tried to repeat the experiment, their gerbils showed no ESP at all.

Despite Duval and Montredon's success, the evidence for animal psi is still shaky. Levy's fraud led many critics to dismiss the whole field, and it will take years of patient, careful research to overcome his influence. And testing scores will have to climb. Too many experiments depend on random behavior, and critics say that's not good enough.

But people who want to forget animal psi will have to explain Helmut Schmidt's cat. Schmidt put the cat in a cold shed during the middle of winter. He also put a 200-watt lamp in the shed and connected the lamp to a machine in a distant building that turned the light off and on. When the cat was in the shed, the light went on much oftener than the timer was set to turn it on, warming the cold animal. When the cat was not in the shed, the light followed the machine-set schedule. Schmidt thinks the cat was showing PK. Perhaps it was.

PART FIVE
Making the Impossible Possible

Alice laughed. "There's no use trying," she said; "one *can't* believe impossible things."

"I daresay you haven't had much practice," said the Queen. "When I was your age, I always did it for half an hour a day. Why sometimes I've believed as many as six impossible things before breakfast."

Lewis Carroll,
Through the Looking-Glass

14

Sheep and Goats

When parapsychologists switched from testing gifted people to testing large groups, they made the change because they thought everyone had some psychic ability. That tiny bit of ESP didn't show when a single person was tested, because most people's scores would hover just above chance; but test a large group, and the combined glimmer of ESP became impressive.

Hundreds of experiments showed that trace of ESP, but it was not big enough to be exciting and it did not convince people who weren't already believers in parapsychology. Besides, it didn't tell us much about the nature of extrasensory perception. The ESP was so weak that parapsychologists found it almost impossible to study.

In every test for parapsychology, some people did better than others. As they watched subjects display traces of telepathy or clairvoyance or PK, researchers wondered if there was any way to tell in advance when a person had psychic talent. They had already noted that some researchers seemed to have better luck with their subjects than others.

J. B. Rhine had only to walk into a lab, it seemed, for the subjects to display psychic ability. Over the years, 20 percent of the people he tested had shown some talent. Yet other researchers, such as John Beloff of Scotland, could take the same experiment that had worked for others and find no traces of psi in any of his subjects. When he came into a lab, psi turned off, as if he had flipped a switch.

If the personality of the researcher was so powerful, perhaps the personality of the subject was important, too. If ESP and PK turned out to be connected with certain kinds of personality, parapsychologists might find the key that would unlock the mystery.

One of the first researchers to work at uncovering the link between personality and psi was Gertrude Schmeidler. During the 1950s, she decided to find out whether her suspicions were true: people who believed in ESP showed more of the elusive ability than disbelievers.

Schmeidler divided the people she tested into two groups: sheep and goats. The sheep were people who said they believed that ESP existed; the goats said it was all nonsense. When she tested her subjects on Zener cards, the sheep made more hits than the goats. She ran eight different experiments and got the same results every time.

In addition, in every experiment except one, the goats missed more often than they should have. It looked as if parapsychologists were right: people who don't believe in

ESP are often psi-missers. When their minds pick up any information by extrasensory methods, they unconsciously sabotage it.

Most other researchers who tried such experiments got the same results as Schmeidler. On several occasions, though, the goats did as well as the sheep. When John Beloff and David Bate worked with children in Edinburgh, the goats tested by Beloff scored well above chance. But Bate's goats psi-missed, just as they were supposed to do.

The pair had similar trouble with believers. They tested a group of supersheep, people who thought they were pretty good at ESP, and found they did worse than regular sheep or goats. Given Beloff's consistent bad luck, perhaps his work does not detract from Schmeidler's.

Goats are not good at predicting the future, either. Milan Ryzl tested eighty people for precognition by asking them to make five hundred guesses as to which of the five Zener symbols would later turn up. None of his eighty subjects showed any signs of precognition, but the dozen goats who pooh-poohed any possibility of ESP did so badly that they seemed to be psi-missing.

A study that used no Zener symbols at all was set up by Thelma Moss and J. A. Gengerelli. They divided 144 people into 72 teams, each consisting of a transmitter and a receiver. The transmitter sat in a soundproof isolation room and watched a large screen. When pictures flashed on the screen, a tape recorder played music and other sounds that intensified the picture's mood. For example, when slides of lions, snakes, and tigers devouring their prey appeared on the screen, the transmitter heard a wild piece of music that included the screams of fierce animals. As the transmitter experienced the sights and sounds, she tried to send her feelings to the receiver.

In another room, twenty feet away, sat the receiver. After he tried to sense the transmitter's message, he looked at a pair of screens. One always showed the pictures the transmitter had seen; the other was entirely different. When the transmitter sent the frightening animals, for example, the second pictures were always a series of abstract paintings that ended with the picture of a tree.

When the receiver guessed right, he sometimes seemed to pick up the content of the picture itself and sometimes merely picked up the picture's mood. Once when pictures of Mary and the baby Jesus were shown to the transmitter, the receiver said, "I get the image of a child. Children. Now it's a cradle rocking. And inside there's a baby with swaddling clothes."

A receiver who seemed to pick up the mood said, "A feeling of calmness . . . serenity . . . elegance . . . lavishness," and reported that he heard music from *My Fair Lady*. He chose the picture of the Madonna and Child instead of a self-portrait by Vincent van Gogh, a famous artist who became insane and cut off his own ear.

Moss and Gengerelli found that goats scored right at chance. They found no psi-missers. Sheep who believed in ESP but didn't think they had any ability did no better. But supersheep, who thought they had ESP themselves, guessed the right pictures much oftener than they should have. The odds against their scores were three hundred to one.

That was good enough, but Moss and Gengerelli found something even more impressive. When they divided their subjects by occupation, they found that artists did better than anyone. Subjects who were creative artists outscored businessmen, housewives, students, psychologists, and even five people who were supposed to be psychics. When a writer, musician, or actor was either the transmitter or the receiver, the scores were so high that there was only 1 chance in 200,000 that they were merely lucky.

Other studies have shown that just dividing people into sheep and goats does not account for the apparent possession of ESP, or the lack of it. Schmeidler herself found that whether or not a person is emotionally stable affects his ESP score. Well-adjusted sheep seem to show stronger signs of ESP than poorly adjusted sheep, while well-adjusted goats psi-miss more than poorly adjusted goats. Apparently people who have emotional problems don't make good psychics.

But adjustment is not enough. Schmeidler also discovered that people with a theoretical cast of mind, those who enjoy speculating on possibilities, do better than those who don't. And, as you might expect, theoretical sheep do well on ESP tests, while theoretical goats are psi-missers.

Hans Eysenck, a British psychologist, tried to make it simple. He believed that extroverts, outgoing people who quickly respond to the world about them, do better at ESP than introverts, quiet, withdrawn people who are primarily concerned with their own thoughts and feelings. The brains of introverts are too alert and active, he believes, and so much goes on inside them, that their inner mental activity keeps them from picking up the mental images of others.

When B. K. Kathamani and K. R. Rao studied teenagers

at English schools in India, they found that Eysenck's predictions held up. In four different studies, the extroverts made better scores than they should have, while the introverts did worse. Back in England, John Randall found that not all extroverts make high scores. Among the English schoolboys he studied, many of the extroverts made extremely low scores. Randall believes they were psi-missing.

As the research went on, it became apparent that more than one aspect of personality was linked to ESP. Kathamani and Rao's studies of teenagers in India helped them develop a picture of the ideal psychic. Such a person, they found, would be good-natured, easygoing, warm and sociable, self-assured, talkative, cheerful, enthusiastic, and adventurous, but tough and not easily upset. In other words, a well-adjusted, realistic extrovert who tends to dominate others. The person who ought to forget mind reading or peering into the future was aloof, suspicious, tense, impatient, submissive, shy, and withdrawn.

Other researchers were trying different personality combinations. Charles Honorton and his coworkers tested groups of people for precognition. They went to an advanced humanities course for seniors at a local high school and talked to them about parapsychology. Then, after the 110 seniors tried to predict a run of Zener cards, the researchers asked them to fill out several personality tests and to make 250 guesses on the order in which the Zener symbols would later show up.

They found that sheep did better than goats, and that people who drew large, free pictures that filled a paper did better than those who drew small careful drawings in one section of the page. But the single best test for ESP ability was creativity. Highly creative people did much better than persons with little or no creativity. That finding fits right in with the work of Moss and Gengerelli.

Over the last twenty-five years, more than a hundred different experiments have been tried. Although from time to time a researcher will find that the poorly adjusted people she tests score higher than the well adjusted, or that the introverts outscore the extroverts, most show the same results. People who believe in ESP, who are well adjusted and outgoing, generally show glimpses of psychic ability.

The low scores of poorly adjusted introverts who don't believe in ESP show the same glimpses. Psi-missing, say parapsychologists, is as strong an evidence for psychic ability as making a high score, and psi-missers are as talented as high scorers.

The key word, however, is *glimpses*. Even after sorting out the most likely people, the tests are not turning up psychics who can read minds, sense remote events, or see into the future. Some would say that the results aren't strong enough to be convincing. Some would argue that because ESP is not supposed to occur, we unconsciously smother any information we get by psychic means. Others believe that ESP is an undeveloped talent, one we don't use because our other senses are so powerful we don't need it. If that is true, perhaps tests of blind or deaf people would turn up stronger evidence for ESP.

The most encouraging news is that almost all the tests point in the same direction. This means that the link between ESP and personality must be taken seriously.

15

Dreams in the Night

Through decades of research, parapsychologists noticed that people who seemed to have ESP or PK often had bad days. They worked best when they felt good and when those around them were sympathetic. It seemed plain that a person's mood affected his or her chances of doing well.

In 1972, Charles Honorton showed how important mood was. He and his coworkers ran ESP tests with two different groups. They treated the first group politely and put them at their ease. With the second group, they were rude and unpleasant and made them feel uncomfortable. The people in the first group scored above chance; the unhappy subjects in the second group became psi-missers.

Even before Honorton showed how important a smile and a friendly greeting could be to the outcome of a parapsychological experiment, others had noticed that high-scoring people seemed to be in a dreamlike state. Rhea White compared the early studies done by Rhine and others with the card-guessing experiments of the 1960s. She pointed out three things.

First, the early experimenters found people who showed much stronger signs of ESP than modern subjects could muster. Second, the people in those early experiments were given plenty of time and encouraged to look inside themselves. Some of them described themselves as feeling detached, abstracted, or relaxed. Modern researchers, afraid of having their experiments criticized, pushed their subjects rapidly through the cards and never bothered to inquire about inner states.

Finally, White stressed the dreamlike state of the high scorers. Rhine, whose subjects so frequently showed ESP, often used the word *trance* as the best description of their appearance. White suggested that those high scorers were not just relaxing, they were tapping "another level of the self," a level not reached by people who give quick guesses about the order of cards.

What White was describing was an *altered state of consciousness*, which researchers often refer to as ASC. When we are awake and going about our daily business, talking, working a math problem, walking, or eating, we are in our ordinary, everyday state. It is the state we connect with being conscious.

But there are other states of consciousness. Strong emotions, sleep, dreams, drugs, hypnosis, and meditation each change our mental state, and we function differently in each one. Among the waking states, a person who is violently angry, one who is daydreaming about his lover, one who is balancing a checkbook, and one who has taken a psychedelic drug are each in a different state of consciousness. All but the person working on his checkbook are in ASCs, and each sees and reacts to the world differently.

If White was right, the search for the secret of ESP should shift to ASCs. This means that researchers would have to become familiar with the electroencephalograph, a machine that reports exactly what the brain is doing. When electrodes are pasted onto a person's scalp, the machine records the tiny pulses of electricity produced by the working brain. The recording, called an electroencephalogram, or an EEG, shows the frequency and strength of each electrical impulse.

As a person shifts from active thought to relaxation to sleep, his EEG reflects the changes in his brain's activity. Shifts in EEG pattern might signal researchers when a person was in a state of consciousness that is receptive to ESP.

Researchers have already begun to study one altered state: dreaming. In 1952, Eugene Aserinsky and Nathaniel Kleitman discovered that during dreams, a person's eyes move rapidly beneath his closed lids. If a dreamer in rapid-eye-movement sleep, called *REM-sleep*, is wakened, he can usually describe his dreams.

People who believed they had experienced telepathy, clairvoyance, or precognition often said that the messages came through while they were sleeping. They dreamed of friends or relatives in trouble or of shipwrecks or other disasters that lay in the future. As many as two-thirds of reported cases of ESP are dreams.

Montague Ullman, a psychoanalyst whose patients often reported what seemed to be psychic dreams, had been interested in dream telepathy for a long time. In the early 1960s, he set up the first laboratory experiments at Maimonides Medical Center in Brooklyn, New York.

Ullman's subjects were chosen on two grounds: they had to be good at remembering their dreams, and they had to be sheep. His plan was to have them go to sleep in the lab's soundproof room, one at a time. Electrodes connected them to a machine in another room that reported their brain wave patterns and eye movements. Each time the EEG told a researcher that the subject was in REM-sleep, he pressed a button to signal the sender, who sat alone in a distant room. The sender then concentrated on a picture, which he had just selected by picking a sealed envelope from a group of twelve. At the end of the REM-sleep period, another researcher wakened the dreamer and taped his or her description of the dream.

After the sleepers had spent a night in the lab, the transcripts of the dreams and all the pictures were sent to a group of judges, who tried to match the dreams to the pictures. Each judge worked by himself. He read the descriptions of the night's dreams and then ranked the paintings from one to twelve, beginning with the one that seemed to him most like the dream.

Not once did all three judges say that the night's dreams were most like the target picture. Each sleeper's dreams varied enough so that they also resembled at least one of the other pictures. Statistically, the experiment was a failure.

But the researchers and the dreamers were excited. One of the sleepers, a psychologist named William Erwin, did dream close enough to his target picture to satisfy the judges and the mathematicians. Some of Erwin's dreams resembled another painting, but at least one of the judges had no trouble making the match, and all agreed that there were strong elements of the target picture in his dreams.

One of the senders, Sol Feldstein, did much better than the others. Out of six tries, Feldstein succeeded in influencing dreams five times. Joyce Plosky, the second sender, was successful three times out of six. In addition, Feldstein's dreamers came closer to the painting on most occasions. It appeared that the sender was as important as the receiver.

One of the problems with such dream experiments showed up on the first night Feldstein worked as a sender. He concentrated on a picture of two fierce dogs, whose teeth showed as they gnawed on hunks of meat. Behind them was a large black rock.

Although the dreamer's reports on her first awakening showed no resemblance to the picture, her second dream was about Black Rock, Vermont, and she told of sitting on a rock at the beach, feeling like a mermaid from Black Rock. In her third dream, she was at a banquet, chewing on a piece of steak. A friend of hers sat nearby, greedily watching the other diners to make sure they didn't get more meat than she did. Her friend's greed was so apparent that the other guests were talking about it.

It seemed that the dreamer transformed the impressions she received, mixing them with other material that was stored in her memory. Everyone is familiar with the way dreams change the stuff of our waking lives, blending past and present, fact and fiction, often dealing with symbols instead of actual events. If dreamers are likely to disguise and distort telepathic impressions that reach them, it will always be difficult to judge the success of an experiment. What seems like ESP to one person will be dismissed as far-fetched by another. A critic is likely to say that you can find a disguised symbol in any dream if you are determined to find it.

A second, similar series the following year did no better than the first. Although the judges said that the dreamers may have picked up something from the target painting six nights out of twelve, they found that the dreams always bore a stronger resemblance to the wrong painting. But when the dreamers themselves looked at a dozen paintings the following morning, they selected the right painting nine times. A dreamer would choose the correct picture and say, "Something — I don't know exactly what — about this target reminds me of my dreams." It would appear that the judges' grading of ESP dream studies are likely to be less impressive than the experiments seem to the people who take part in them.

The Maimonides team did better when they concentrated on William Erwin, who had done so well in the first experiment. With Sol Feldstein as the sender, Erwin dreamed in the lab for seven nights. This time he made three direct hits; all the judges agreed that there was a complete match between his dreams and the night's picture. On three other nights, they found strong elements of the target picture in his dreams, but said that they seemed closer to some of the other paintings in the pool of pictures. On only one night did Erwin fail completely. The odds were a hundred to one against such results.

Two years later, Erwin came back for another eight nights. This time, the sender not only concentrated on a picture but acted it out.

One night, for example, Feldstein concentrated on a Japanese print that showed a man with an umbrella struggling against a pelting rain. Each time Erwin entered REM-sleep, Feldstein picked up a toy parasol and took a shower. On the night that Feldstein tried to send a photograph of a display that showed four Confederate soldiers loading a cannon, he played with toy rubber soldiers. Erwin outdid himself. This time there were six direct hits and no complete misses. The odds were ten thousand to one against that kind of dreaming.

Another champion dreamer was Robert Van de Castle, a psychologist who was interested in parapsychology and who headed his own dream lab at the University of Virginia. Van de Castle easily fitted the sheep requirement, and he believed he had had telepathic dreams in the past. At Maimonides he dreamed for eight nights. The judges said he made direct hits on five of those nights and missed completely twice. Van de Castle, on looking at the paintings, said he had hit six times. Even if we stick with the judges, there was only one chance in twenty-five hundred that the dreams were accidental.

Like other dreamers, Van de Castle transformed the pictures in his dreams. One night, the sender concentrated on a picture of three men sitting outside a primitive shelter in India. The men all wore hats of some kind, one was playing a stringed instrument, and another was holding a bow and arrows. The third had a riflelike stick over his shoulder and a bundle wrapped in cloth at his feet. In the background was a stake with a rope tied around it.

That night Van de Castle had six dreams; two of them had a western setting, with cowboys and guns. Four of the dreams included ropes or strings or cord. The first dream started with a bedroll, then moved to three men wearing berets and holding rifles. Van de Castle got the word *gunslinger,* and reported that the setting was either foreign or rural or western. The second dream included cowboys with guns, country music, and three or four coils of rope that ended with a hanged man. Both the judges and Van de Castle rated this as a direct hit.

The dreamer apparently picked up the weapons, the musical instrument, the cloth bundle, and the three hatted men, but the strings on the instrument, the bowstring, and the rope combined to overpower his dreams. In a third dream, a drowned person was pulled from the water by a rope, and yet another included a hammock with lots of "suspended strings."

Dreaming in the lab was so successful that the next try involved long-distance telepathy. Stanley Krippner asked the rock group the Grateful Dead to use their entire audience as senders, just as the Holy Modal Rounders had done the year before. He arranged to have two subjects; both had done well in earlier dream experiments. But he told the Grateful Dead about only one of the dreamers:

Malcolm Bessent. The second dreamer was known only to the team at Maimonides.

Bessent slept at the lab, where he could be awakened during REM-sleep. The other dreamer, Felicia Parise, slept at her apartment, and a researcher called her every ninety minutes during the night to ask about her dreams.

Slides asked the audience to concentrate on Bessent. They said, "Try using your ESP to 'send' this picture to Malcolm Bessent. He will try to dream about the picture. Try to 'send' it to him. Malcolm Bessent is now at the Maimonides Dream Laboratory in Brooklyn." Then, while the Grateful Dead played, the slide stayed on the screen for fifteen minutes.

To be sure that neither dreamer could know beforehand what picture would be sent, two slides were chosen each night from a pool of fourteen. Just before the experiment began, the evening's slide was selected by the flip of a coin.

For six nights the Grateful Dead's audience, two thousand strong, concentrated on sending a picture to Bessent, who was forty-five miles from the Capitol Theater in Portchester, New York. On four of the nights, Bessent made direct hits, his dreams reflecting the slides in a way that satisfied the judges. Parise hit only once, on the last night of the series.

Apparently, two thousand senders are no better than one, even if many are in an altered state. According to Krippner, some of the audience had taken psychedelic drugs before the concert; most of the others were in an ASC simply from the music. But Bessent's success indicates that the intention of the sender may indeed make a difference in telepathy.

Bessent was even able to dream about things to come. In an attempt at precognition, he dreamed in the lab about something that would happen the next day. When he wakened each morning, the experimenters put him through an experience that had not been planned until he finished his night's dreams. Krippner, who designed the experience, did not know what Bessent had dreamed. Again, the success was too good to be luck.

In all, the team at Maimonides ran a dozen studies. Nine of them were strikingly successful. The remaining three, although they included some apparently successful nights, were failures. Whatever hits the dreamer made could be attributed to chance.

But one of the things critics insist on is that other experimenters, using the same techniques, get the same results. Most who have tried to repeat the success at Maimonides have failed.

Robert Van de Castle has worked with two other experimenters. When Calvin Hall tested him, Van de Castle again produced telepathic dreams. But when he went to David Foulkes's Wyoming laboratory, he failed. This was a serious blow to parapsychologists' hopes, but there may be an explanation.

At Maimonides, the experiment was run by sheep, and Van de Castle later said he was treated like a "visiting sultan." He was highly motivated. Each night at the lab meant a trip of over a thousand miles. Psychologists have found that when a person's will to succeed is strong, his chances increase.

Finally, at Maimonides Van de Castle chose two of the

senders, both young women he found attractive. Each night before he dreamed, he spent time getting to know them and trying to set up a mood that would encourage a telepathic bond. As Adrian Parker has pointed out, in Wyoming the belief in ESP was not as strong, no red carpet was rolled out, the experimenters were pressed for time, and Van de Castle did not have the same rapport with the senders. The wrong mood has wrecked other tries at ESP.

Dreams are only one kind of ASC. Some researchers have taken the Maimonides experiments as a signal to study other altered states.

16

The Wandering Mind

Say the word *hypnosis* and most of us think of the theater. For decades, persuading people to bark like dogs or to carry out silly commands has kept this altered state at the level of hocus-pocus. But hypnosis also has a serious role. Some doctors and dentists use it in place of anesthesia, and some psychologists use it to help their patients change bad habits. Recently, hypnosis has helped witnesses recall details of crimes.

Nearly a hundred years ago, hypnosis was first linked with ESP. In France, a hypnotized woman was told to visit a distant laboratory. Sitting in the room with Pierre Janet, the hypnotist, she described a fire in the lab. She was right. The lab was blazing; it seemed that while hypnotized she had been clairvoyant.

Another time she was asked to tell what a certain man

was doing. He was, she reported, burning his hand with a brown liquid. Again she was right. At the time of her hypnotic clairvoyance, the man spilled bromine, a reddish brown liquid, and burned himself.

There is no way to investigate these reports, but they were given to us by Charles Richet, a French scientist who won the Nobel Prize for medicine. It was his lab that was on fire, and there is no reason to doubt his word.

Hypnosis is an odd state, because unlike dreaming, there is no way to look at EEGs or other bodily measures and tell when a person is hypnotized. Some psychologists, like Theodore Barber, say that a "hypnotized" person is merely someone who has an intense wish to succeed at whatever task the hypnotist gives him. Many other psychologists agree that hypnosis exists, that some people are easily hypnotized, and that, while in the state, they are highly responsive to the suggestions of others.

But suggesting to hypnotized people that they are telepathic or clairvoyant will not make them so. Sometimes hypnotized people do worse at guessing Zener cards than when they are in their normal state. When Charles Honorton and Stanley Krippner looked closely at two dozen different hypnosis experiments, they found that people who already do well at ESP do even better when they are hypnotized, but people who do poorly do even worse.

Many of those experiments used Zener cards. Krippner used hypnosis in a different way. He and his coworkers hypnotized eight people, brought them out of their hypnotic state, and had them take a nap. While they were hypnotized and again while they were napping, someone concentrated on a picture, trying to send them the content. Before they left the lab, they described their imaginings while hypnotized and their dreams during the nap. The contents of the picture had gotten through to them.

Eight other people, who merely relaxed in the lab, had no luck then. But that night, in their own homes, some of the unhypnotized people had dreams that resembled the picture. Hypnosis seemed to drop barriers, letting the picture come into awareness. The unhypnotized people weren't aware that they had received the picture until later, when they dreamed.

When Honorton used two altered states, combining hypnosis with dreams, he got clairvoyance. In 1972, he brought sixty women into the Maimonides lab and hypnotized half of them. One at a time, they were placed in a darkened room and told that they would sleep for five minutes, dreaming about a picture that was carefully wrapped and sealed in three thicknesses of heavy paper. At the end of five minutes, they would wake and tell Honorton about the dream.

The other thirty women were also taken into a darkened room, but they were not hypnotized. Instead, they were instructed to daydream for five minutes about the wrapped picture and then to describe their thoughts.

Before any of the women went into the room, each took a test that told researchers how easily she could be hypnotized. Both groups included ten women who entered a hypnotic trance with little effort.

The daydreamers failed at clairvoyance. Their daydreams bore little resemblance to the sealed pictures. Hypnosis had a different effect. Although most of this group also failed, some of the ten easily hypnotized women had dreams that picked up the paintings.

One young woman had her hypnotic dream while seated beside a wrapped print of El Greco's painting *The Adoration of the Shepherds*. This painting shows the baby Jesus in his mother's arms. Shepherds and angels are gathered around the pair, who sit beneath an arched roof. Green shrubbery grows in the background. When this woman wakened, she described her dream as, "The Virgin Mary. A statue and Jesus Christ. An old church with two pillars overgrown with grass by the church entrance. The Virgin Mary was holding Jesus as a baby."

Another woman, Felicia Parise, dreamed beside a wrapped copy of Hiroshige's painting *The Kinryuszan Temple*. This Japanese picture shows a red and gold lantern hanging from a temple doorway. Through the door, one looks down a snow-covered lane. When Parise woke from her hypnotic sleep, she reported, "A lot of things — a car going by. A room with party decorations. Thought I saw people, but there wasn't anyone there. Then everything went white. I saw a gold chest, like a pirate's chest, but shining and new. No decorations on the floor, but they were on the ceilings and walls. There was a table with things on it. Red balloons, red punch bowls."

Parise told Honorton that her dream reminded her of her sixteenth birthday party, which had been decorated with Japanese lanterns. According to Krippner, she brought a snapshot of that party to the lab for the researchers to see. The photograph strongly resembled the painting she had tried to dream about. As in the EEG-monitored dream experiments, the sleeper's mind seemed to mix the painting with memories.

Honorton asked the dreamers to describe their hypnotic trance and found that those who reported deep trances also had dreams that resembled the pictures. The greater the shift in the dreamer's state of consciousness, the more striking the resemblance. The chances were one in twenty-five that the suggestible women's dreams were only lucky resemblances to the picture.

Three other teams of researchers have conducted hypnotic dream studies, and all reported some success. Adrian Parker and John Beloff ran two such studies. The first worked; the second did not.

Parker says that the dreamers in the first group were acquaintances who were interested in the project and who wanted it to succeed. The dreamers in the second group were volunteers who didn't care whether the study failed or succeeded. If mood and attitude are as important in ESP as some experiments indicate, the difference could account for the failure of the second study. It is just this unmeasurable, personal quality that makes ESP so difficult to pin down.

Once researchers began to verify the ability of the Indian holy men to slow their hearts, to feel no pain, or to change their brain wave patterns at will, work with ASCs shifted away from hypnosis.

Yogis alter their own state of consciousness by meditating, focusing their attention on a phrase, which they repeat over and over, or on their breath as it enters and leaves their bodies. A person who is meditating is in a relaxed state that would seem favorable for ESP. Indeed, yogis and other meditators are not surprised by ESP, and many say that it naturally accompanies the practice of meditation.

In one experiment, meditators tried their hands at ESP once a week for six months. Each came to the lab, meditated for half an hour, then stuck his hand through a curtain and attempted to choose the square on a checkerboard that researchers already had selected as the target. At other times, the meditator tried to receive a photograph that a researcher was sending him.

Not all the meditators were successful. But Karlis Osis and Edwin Bokert interviewed them and found that the psi-missers and the psi-hitters were different from the meditators whose scores showed nothing. Those with unusual scores felt a sense of openness and said that meditation took them beyond themselves, so that they felt some sort of mingling with the universe. All the people tested by Osis and Bokert were experienced meditators.

Gertrude Schmeidler used people who had never meditated. She tested six graduate students for ESP, then had an expert show them how to meditate. The students meditated, then took the ESP test again. Before they heard the expert, they showed not a glimmer of ESP. But after they meditated, they made more hits than they should have. However, two runs with six students can't show that meditation turns on ESP, because with so few guesses, luck is a strong possibility.

Another group of meditators was not successful. These

people signed up for a course on meditation and learned to alter their consciousness by focusing their attention on a phrase, which they repeated to themselves as they meditated.

The group as a whole showed no ESP, but William Roll and Gerald Solfvin asked each person to rate his feelings before and after he meditated. When they compared the self-rating to ESP scores, they found that the meditators who made hits said they felt uncomfortable, had no sense of inner peace, and had not the slightest feeling of mingling with the universe. In addition, they reported a lot of day-dreaming. This time the people who were poorest at meditation did best at ESP.

Roll and Solfvin kept working. In 1976 they reported that another group of nine people learned to meditate, then came to the lab for ten days, where they tried to pick up the subject of a sealed picture as they meditated.

Again, they found no strong relationship between meditation and ESP. Any success had to do not with an ASC, but with the meditators' feelings about the target picture. When they liked the subject of the picture, they seemed to make hits. When they disliked the subject, they began psi-missing. Roll and Solfvin are still in search of the link they believe exists between ESP and meditation.

A link ought to exist. When people talk about the way they feel while meditating, their words sound like those used by persons who score extremely high on ESP tests. They also sound like people in psychology labs who have learned to control their brain waves.

About ten years ago, in 1967, researchers in California

began using a process called *biofeedback* to teach people to control their brain waves. In San Francisco, Joe Kamiya pasted silver electrodes to his subjects' scalps and attached them to an electroencephalograph. Each time their brains produced a pattern of waves called "alpha," a tone sounded. When their brains stopped producing alpha, the tone turned off. Before long, although they were not sure just how they did it, these people could produce alpha waves whenever they wished.

People who are producing alpha say they are "not thinking" or "letting the mind wander" or "feeling the heart beat." Whenever they recite the alphabet, try to work a math problem, or imagine seeing visual images, the alpha turns off as if they had flipped a switch.

Some researchers have turned from meditation to measuring alpha. The people they test can produce alpha by any means they like, and some use meditation.

In 1972, Robert Morris and his coworkers hooked electrodes to Lalsingh Harribance, who had made impressive scores on clairvoyance and PK tests. This time, while a researcher in another room looked at pictures of people, Harribance tried to guess whether they were male or female. Without any ESP at all, he should have guessed right half the time. He did much, much better, and when he was at his best, making hit after hit, the EEG showed that he was spending the most time in alpha and that his output of alpha was rising sharply.

Charles Honorton believes that the shift in alpha production is more important than the alpha wave itself. He believes that when a person's state of consciousness makes a large change, and does it quickly, that he is in an ideal state for ESP.

Honorton himself used biofeedback to train twenty-three individuals so they could turn alpha on and off. These people told Honorton and his colleagues how they felt when switching in or out of an alpha state. Sure enough, they were more relaxed and paying less attention to the outside world when the EEG was recording alpha. And the people who reported the most relaxation, the least attention to their surroundings, and the greatest shift in consciousness did best at clairvoyance.

More than a dozen studies have explored the possibility that alpha waves make ESP more likely. In some of the experiments, lots of alpha meant high scores. In others, people who produced little alpha did better than those who produced a lot. Most of the studies, however, showed that as the amount of alpha begins to increase, scores on ESP tests go up.

One researcher tried combining two promising approaches in one experiment. Edwin May built a psi-testing machine that produced more than one kind of feedback. Like other machines, it told a person when he or she made a hit, but it also gave biofeedback. The person being tested also knew when he was producing alpha waves.

Working with Charles Honorton, May tested Ingo Swann, a psychic who has a reputation for making high scores on ESP tests. Swann tried to influence the machine 29,000 times and came up with a score that showed some PK. As he worked with the machine, his score got better, which indicates that he may have learned from the feedback.

Before accepting Swann's score as an indication of PK, May and Honorton tested other people. Just an hour after Swann left the lab, they had others try to influence the machine 300,000 times. No psi-hitting, no psi-missing. The scores were right at chance.

May and Honorton used the same machine to test ten people who were experienced meditators. The meditators knew when they made a hit, but got no biofeedback. They did even better than Swann, showing strong evidence of PK. When they were asked to psi-miss, their scores dipped. This time, however, scores got worse as the experiment continued. The decline effect took over even though they got feedback on each hit.

Another way to alter a person's state of consciousness is to cut off the sensations that normally come from the outside world. Psychologists call this *sensory deprivation*, and some experiments have shown that people in this condition often see things that aren't there or feel as if they have left their bodies. Their brains also produce a lot of alpha waves.

Hundreds of years ago, witches used a sort of sensory deprivation to enter an altered state. They would take a drug, wrap themselves in a sheath, and climb into a cage that was suspended from the limb of a tree. As the cradle swung, the witch, in her ASC, believed that she had left her body and had traveled to a meeting of her fellow witches.

A modern witch's cradle has been used in telepathy experiments. After putting dark goggles over their eyes and plugs in their ears, Charles Honorton and his coworkers put thirty people into a metal swing and asked them to rate their state of consciousness every five minutes. During their last ten minutes in the swing, they tried to pick up a painting that was being sent to them by a researcher in another room.

Most people who reported strong shifts in consciousness apparently read the researcher's mind. After the experience, they were able to select the painting that had been sent when shown a group of eight paintings. Those who reported little or no shift in consciousness chose the right picture less often than they should have by luck alone.

Honorton now uses another kind of sensory deprivation to look for ESP. He asks people to look through a ganzfeld, which is simply a Ping-Pong ball cut in half, with each half covering one eye. Instead of putting plugs in their ears, he uses earphones that transmit "white noise," rushing, roaring sounds that keep the person from hearing anything meaningful.

His first experiments were very like the one with the witch's cradle, but with a surprise twist. Half the time, the sender saw a picture for only a split second — so short a time that he was not conscious he had even seen it. The rest of the time he gazed steadily at the picture he was trying to send. When the sender literally didn't know what he had seen, the person who could neither see nor hear often picked up the target painting. When the sender looked at the picture for a long time, the scores dropped to chance.

Honorton and S. Harper tried to repeat the experiment. This time the split-second glance at the pictures didn't work. The whole group scored at chance.

With James Terry, Honorton recently tried another set of

experiments. This time he asked college students to relax and think out loud during the thirty minutes they spent in the ganzfeld. For ten of those thirty minutes, a student in another room tried to send the contents of a Viewmaster reel.

In twenty-seven tries, the young men looking through the Ping-Pong balls picked up the pictures twenty-one times. One team made a perfect score: seven hits out of seven tries.

Once, the sender was viewing a reel that portrayed the adventures of "Lancelot Link, Secret Chimp," in which chimpanzees dressed in trench coats act out a detective story. Before the sender looked at the reel, the subject came up with, "a chimpanzee from *2001* jumping up and down." As the sender stared at the chimps' antics, the subject said he saw "apes and prehuman life styles." After the reel was put away, the subject continued to describe: "The images of prehistoric dogs, prehuman apemen, what a rough existence they must have had. An image of a family friend who is a policeman, blue uniform and badge."

Note that *before* the sender saw Lancelot Link, the subject was thinking of chimps. This sort of thing happened again and again. If the reel was selected before the attempt at telepathy began, then the subject appears to have been clairvoyant. If the reel was not selected until the sender was ready to look at it, the experiment seems to have included precognition.

Honorton's second set of similar ganzfeld studies was just as successful. Other researchers have done ganzfeld studies. Some have shown ESP; some have not. But information seems to pass between the sender and receiver too often to give up this kind of work. Honorton believes that some of the experiments were failures because the receivers didn't look through the ganzfeld long enough before they were tested.

Others may have failed because the researchers paid little attention to the mood of their subjects. At Maimonides, a good deal of effort goes into establishing a feeling of relaxed confidence. The experimenter is warm and friendly, and tells the subject that while he'll probably be successful, it's OK if he isn't. Paintings and posters on the walls and stereo music help soften the cold, scientific atmosphere of the lab.

For some time, Honorton has bet that a combination of sensory deprivation and rapid shifts of consciousness is the best way to track down ESP. He seems to be right.

17

The Problem of Uri Geller

Most people have heard of Uri Geller. The young Israeli has had more publicity than any psychic in history. He has appeared on television programs, has written his autobiography, and at least four books have been written about him.

Some people believe he is a gifted psychic, good at telepathy, clairvoyance, and psychokinesis, able to bend keys, start stopped watches, and drive a car while blindfolded. Other people say he is a fake. The truth is hard to come by.

Geller was born in Israel in 1946. In his native country, he was a stage performer whose act included mind reading and describing, while blindfolded, whatever people drew on a blackboard. Geller said that his dazzling effects were the result of his paranormal powers. Many Israelis believed him; others did not and claimed that Shipi Shtrang, who always sat near the front of the theater and who still goes everywhere with Geller, passed him the information that made him seem psychic.

His act was either pure parapsychology, a combination of parapsychology and magician's tricks, or the performance of a skilled magician. We simply do not know. But whatever it was, Geller became immensely popular in theaters and nightclubs.

Then he ran into trouble. At the height of his fame, he gave a picture of himself and film actress Sophia Loren to the Israeli papers. The picture turned out to be a fake. Sometime later, Geller came to the United States. He says that he left Israel so that his powers could be tested by scientists. Others say that after the picture appeared he had a hard time finding work.

Whatever the reason, since he came to this country he has been tested in several labs, has appeared on all the major TV talk shows, and has given stage performances across the land. The results have been varied.

When Geller shows off his skills, the performance is usually confusing. He tends to flit from one feat to the next, picking up keys, starting watches, copying drawings, going back to the keys. It is impossible to watch him carefully or set up any controls. Whenever he succeeds, he seems as excited and surprised as his audience.

Andrew Weil, a physician, visited Geller in his New York apartment. Weil had seen Geller perform before an audience in California and had been present at an earlier New York gathering when the psychic seemed to show clairvoyance and PK. On these occasions, he reproduced drawings he had not seen and bent keys, rings, and forks.

When Weil arrived that evening, five reporters were in the apartment. He could tell from the bent spoons and keys on the table that Geller had already been at work. The journalists told Weil that Geller had started a stopped watch and caused a ring to materialize in midair and drop onto a table.

After some talk about flying saucers and Geller's psychic powers, one of the reporters noticed that something had happened to a watch Geller had started. It was still running, but the hands had jumped ahead four hours.

Weil took a broken watch from his shirt pocket and found that it, too, was running. Geller claimed that he was responsible. When Weil laid out several keys and a bolt for the psychic to work on, he inadvertently bumped the table. The bolt began to roll. Excitedly, Geller claimed that he had moved the steel object.

Now Geller tried to bend one of Weil's keys. He picked it up, stroked it, but nothing happened. A group of men from a local TV station arrived. Geller put down the key and tried to reproduce a figure drawn by one of the men. He failed. Again he tried to bend the key but could not.

While Geller turned his head, the man from the TV station drew two intersecting circles. Geller tried to reproduce the drawing and came up with two circles side by side, then with a small circle inside a large one. He still could not bend the key.

Later that night, the man told the TV audience that Geller had drawn two intersecting circles, transforming the near-miss into a hit. Once again, memory had distorted an event and shown the unreliability of eyewitness reports.

When the two men were alone, Geller tried again to bend the key with the power of his mind. He failed. After several attempts, he piled Weil's pocketknife and belt buckle onto a heap of keys. Weil stretched his hand over the pile and Geller laid his hand on top. Weil felt a throb and looked at the objects. The belt buckle was unchanged, but Geller noticed a bend in one of the keys — a bend so slight that Weil at first failed to see it. Geller worked on the key some more. The bend grew sharper. The psychic became excited and hugged Weil.

When Weil left, Geller walked him to the elevator. Just as they parted, Weil's steel bolt struck Geller on the arm and bounced to the floor. Geller claimed to have transported it by PK — without being aware of what he had done.

The performance convinced Weil that Geller's powers were genuine. His faith lasted until he visited the Amazing Randi, a professional magician. Randi bent a key and a nail, reproduced drawings that were in sealed envelopes, and duplicated several of Geller's other feats. Weil changed his mind, certain that Geller was a fake.

Based on this episode, Geller's powers seem questionable. But a casual performance in a private home or on a stage can never settle the problem of psychic powers. It is always easy to cheat, and Randi convinced Weil that Geller had tricked him. Only laboratory tests will ever determine whether Geller is a gifted psychic or a clever magician. Such tests are more difficult to devise than one would expect.

Several labs have studied Geller. Russell Targ and

Harold Puthoff of Stanford Research Institute had two tries. In the first, they spent five weeks watching Geller bend spoons, tell which of ten sealed cans held water or a steel ball, reproduce drawings, change the readings on compassed and laboratory instruments, and call the fall of dice. He passed with flying colors, and his performance was filmed.

But Targ and Puthoff refused to say that their film had captured a psychic at work. Although it looked genuine, they pointed out that there had been a chance for Geller to cheat. A concealed piece of metal too small for a detector to pick up could deflect a compass. The spoons bent only when the researchers relaxed the conditions under which Geller was to bend them, and only when the camera was not running. Although Geller's publicity claimed he could bend metal without touching it, the spoons bent only when they were in Geller's hands. As Targ and Puthoff point out, under such conditions strong fingers could bend the utensils. The sealed cans are a standard magician's trick.

But Targ and Puthoff were convinced that Geller had something. A year later they brought him back to their lab. This time the conditions were strict, more scientific.

First, they put Geller inside a double-walled steel room. Next they chose a target by opening a dictionary and picking the first noun on the page that could be illustrated. The word was *fuse,* so a researcher drew a firecracker. He taped the picture to the outside of the steel room and turned on a microphone that picked up any sounds from inside.

They were ready to begin. Geller's job was to reproduce

the picture that hung on the wall, a picture he couldn't possibly see. First Geller drew a bald man with a long neck, then the head and neck of a giraffelike animal. He said he saw "a cylinder with noise coming out" and drew a drum, wrote "pow" and added several other small objects.

The second word was *bunch*. The researcher drew a bunch of grapes and posted the picture. Geller said he saw "drops of water," then "pure circles." Finally, he said he had it and drew a cluster with exactly the same number of grapes as were in the drawing.

For the next test, Geller went back into the room and a researcher, who was sitting in an office a half mile away, drew a picture of a devil holding a pitchfork. Geller concentrated for thirty minutes and then made three drawings. All had religious themes and the last included a forklike object.

Now Geller came out of the steel room and an experimenter went in. The experimenter drew a picture of the solar system. Geller thought a moment, said "Space," and drew a rocketship speeding through the solar system.

When the researchers tried pure clairvoyance, the experiment failed completely. A scientist who was not part of the team came early to the lab, drew a picture of a rabbit, locked it inside the double-walled room, and left. Geller was brought to the lab and asked to draw the picture. He could not.

Targ and Puthoff put Geller back into the special room and hooked electrodes to him in order to see what happened to his brain waves when he attempted ESP. Because of the electrodes, Geller had to sit quietly while he attempted to receive the pictures posted outside the room. The researchers drew first a tree and then an envelope. Geller failed both times.

For Geller's next test, the psychic went back into the double-walled room and the researchers moved from the adjoining lab into the next room. Now they were farther from Geller and an extra wall was between them. The researchers drew a camel. Geller drew a horse.

The researchers came back into the lab and drew the Golden Gate Bridge. Geller, still inside the steel-walled room, drew some curved lines, rather like a rainbow, and put some squares beneath. He said he didn't know what the picture was, but it resembled an abstract bridge.

The researchers drew a seagull in flight. After only a moment, Geller said he saw a swan flying over a hill. He drew a flying bird.

Two judges, who were not part of the experiment, matched the ten sets of drawings with the targets. They made no mistakes. Targ and Puthoff were satisfied that Geller was telepathic. His drawings were too close to the target pictures to be accidental; they could not figure out how he could be cheating.

However, they were not yet convinced that he was clairvoyant. The one experiment in which no person knew the subject of the picture was a complete failure. In every other case, Geller could have picked the information from someone's mind.

In order to test the psychic for clairvoyance, they moved him to the Engineering Building, where they could use computers to provide the targets. That way, there would be no minds for Geller to read.

Again Geller sat in a double-walled room; this time the walls were of copper screen. A program that had been fed into the computer drew a kite on the face of a TV screen. Geller was told that the picture had been drawn. The researchers waited. Then Geller asked someone to call the computer room and ask whether the picture was that of an object or a geometric design. The computer room replied that it was an object.

When Geller came out of the room, he said that he wouldn't try; he couldn't get the picture. But before he emerged, he had made two sketches. The first was a square with crossed lines drawn inside; it resembled the kite drawn by the computer. The second showed triangular airplanes.

With Geller back in the copper cage, Targ and Puthoff tried two more computer experiments. In the first, a church was drawn, then stored in the computer's memory. Geller failed, although one of his drawings had protrusions that resembled the church cross and steeple. In the second, an arrow-pierced heart was left on the TV screen with the light turned so low that it was invisible. Geller got the arrow but not the heart.

Neither of these last two experiments tested Geller's clairvoyance. Although neither Targ nor Puthoff knew what was in the picture, several people in the room did know what the computer had drawn. Other clairvoyance experiments failed.

An artist drew one hundred pictures, which were placed in double envelopes along with a piece of black cardboard. The pictures were divided into groups of twenty. On three separate days, a group of twenty envelopes was brought out and Geller tried to draw the pictures within. Each day, he made several drawings but said that he wouldn't try to reproduce the pictures. Nothing he drew seemed right to him. When his drawings were compared to the targets, his matches were no better than chance.

In another set of experiments, a researcher took one of a pair of dice and placed it in a steel box. Then he shook the box and asked Geller to write down the number he thought was on top. Geller was right eight times out of ten. This time his clairvoyance seemed to have worked, for no one knew the answer until the box was opened.

Targ and Puthoff also tried a long-distance experiment. They telephoned the East Coast and asked a scientist to draw a picture. He drew two peaked mountains and a sun. Geller drew two arches and a circle, with a trainlike object running through them. In another East Coast telephone experiment, a different scientist drew a cross section of the brain. Geller began by writing words on his paper: medical, organic, living, aviation, architecture. Then he made two drawings. The first was so complex that Targ and Puthoff couldn't describe it. The second looked vaguely like a cross section of living material, but the resemblance was not close.

Did Targ and Puthoff prove that Geller is psychic? They believe that he certainly has shown telepathic powers and some clairvoyance. But they are willing to go no farther.

The major problem with their experiments is that — from the descriptions they have given — only one meets the rigid standards that a number of critics demand. That one, the hundred pictures sealed in double envelopes,

Geller failed spectacularly. When the Geller report was published in the British scientific magazine *Nature,* the English experts pointed out that Targ and Puthoff may well have set up conditions that allowed cheating.

Some American parapsychologists agree with them. Targ and Puthoff's description of the experiments has been called "incomplete and vague." One parapsychologist complained that the paper omitted so much important information that no parapsychological journal would have published it. Because of this, Geller's display of ESP has to be marked "maybe." Other parapsychologists, however, say that the experiments have convinced them that Geller is genuine.

Geller is best known for his key and spoon bending. Metal objects that are brought near him seem to change shape, at times while he is holding them, but often when they are merely in the same room. Some critics say that Geller distracts people's attention, then quickly bends the key in his powerful hands, against his impressive belt buckle, the leg of a chair, or the edge of a table. Others say that he substitutes an already bent key he has hidden on his person. Still others claim that he secretly rubs a chemical onto the key that weakens the metal so that it bends or breaks easily. Magicians are familiar with all these techniques.

But on a couple of occasions, Geller has bent or broken metal objects in ways that the critics cannot account for. In 1973, he visited the Naval Surface Weapons Center in Silver Spring, Maryland. There, engineer Eldon Byrd decided to give him the ultimate test. Byrd had two pieces of nitinol wire, a rare metal alloy that at the time was made only at the Weapons Center. The nickel and titanium alloy, which is used for satellite antennas, has a memory. No matter how much it is bent, dipping it in boiling water makes it spring back to its original shape.

Byrd held a wire between his hands and Geller put his thumb and finger over the center and began to rub. He rubbed for twenty seconds, said he felt a lump, and quit. When he took his fingers away, the wire had a kink in it.

Byrd plunged the wire into boiling water. To his surprise, the wire did not straighten out. Instead, it bent further, until it forced a sharp V. Byrd held a lighted match over the kink, but the bend stayed as sharp as ever.

After Geller left the lab, other scientists took over. They put the bent wire in a vacuum chamber and ran electricity through it until it glowed. The wire straightened out — as it should — but when it cooled the kink returned — as it shouldn't.

Using the point of a screwdriver, Byrd bent another piece of nitinol wire. But in order to bend the wire as sharply and as permanently as Geller had done, he had to use pliers and heat the wire with a Bunsen burner. Byrd also tried using chemicals to soften the wire so that he could make the kink with his bare hands. But it didn't work; the wire was too strong.

Twice Geller returned to the lab, and twice more he made permanent bends in nitinol wire, bends that can be made only by heating the metal to 932°F. None of the metal experts at the lab could explain how the psychic did it.

Many researchers say that this performance with nitinol is the strongest evidence that the young psychic has metal-bending PK. But John Wilhelm is not convinced. He points out that those who are convinced also believe that at that time nitinol could be obtained only from the Navy. Not so, says Wilhelm. When Geller was putting kinks in nitinol wire, anyone could order it from a popular scientific catalog and also get a ninety-six-page book that explained all the properties of the alloy. A company in Ohio, says Wilhelm, was also selling nitinol.

If Geller knew the kind of wire Byrd was going to use as a test, it would have been a simple matter to substitute a pre-bent wire for Byrd's sample. Before Geller bent the wire, he refused to work on an inch-long piece of nitinol that was 3⁄8 inch square. So we are still unable to say firmly that here, at least, Geller showed genuine PK.

Much of Geller's key-bending takes place when no one is looking at the key. Either it is laid aside or it is covered by someone's hand or observers have their attention momentarily diverted. But William E. Cox watched a key bend under convincing circumstances.

The key, which he brought himself, was a safety-deposit blank. That is, it was a key that had not yet been cut to fit a specific lock. Cox, who is a magician as well as a parapsychologist, chose a keyblank because he wanted to be sure that Geller did not switch keys on him. He thought it unlikely that Geller would have such a key.

Geller bent the key when it was lying on a glass coffee table. Cox pressed his finger lightly on one end of the key, using a light touch so that Geller could not use the pressure to help bend it. Cox also placed a mirror beneath the table so that he could watch the underside of the key. In less than a minute, Geller's stroking bent the key. At no time did Cox, who was never more than eighteen inches from the key, take his eyes from it.

Cox was even more impressed when Geller started his watch. Making stopped watches run is a favorite trick of magicians, but anyone can do it. Stopped watches begin to tick whenever they are moved or jarred. Some run for only a few seconds, others for half an hour, and if the watch-spring is broken at a certain position, a watch may run for as long as twelve hours.

Cox prepared his watch in a special way. Ten minutes before he went to see Geller, he opened the back of the watch, set the regulator at Fast, and jammed the balance wheel with a folded strip of aluminum foil. Although the watch was not broken, it could not run.

Geller picked up the watch, shook it, opened the back lid — but not the inner lid — and closed it. Within thirty seconds he had the watch running. Cox took it back, opened the back lid, and pried open the inner lid. The regulator had moved from Fast to Slow, and the piece of foil no longer jammed the balance wheel. He cannot explain it.

The main problem with Cox's account is that he wrote it after he left Geller, depending on his memory. Such descriptions are often distorted, as was the TV newsman's description of Geller's circle drawing. Cox's experience cannot be accepted as proof of Geller's powers.

Cox says that if Geller is not a psychic, he's "a better ma-

gician than any professional twice his age." Other parapsychologists, like Charles Tart, believe that Geller is a
magician most of the time, but that he *occasionally* shows
genuine psychic powers.

Most magicians are more skeptical. They know that they
can duplicate Geller's feats. Some have even passed themselves off to researchers or students of parapsychology as
psychics. The Amazing Randi gave as impressive a performance to the editors of *Psychic News* as Geller gave
for Cox.

Some people say they have caught Geller cheating. According to Wilhelm, the list is long and includes Wilhelm
himself, the Amazing Randi, photographer Yael Joel,
Geller's former girlfriend Hannah Shtrang, and Puthoff and
Targ. Wilhelm also says that Geller has, on several occasions, admitted that he sometimes cheats.

There was a chance to end the confusion. Charles
Honorton invited Geller to come to his laboratory in
Brooklyn. Honorton's tests are so tough that the Amazing
Randi refused to try any of Geller's tricks there. Three
times Geller agreed to be tested by Honorton but never
kept his appointments. Randi says Geller will never show
up. Honorton, tired of wasting time and money preparing
for Geller's visit, quit inviting him. It looks as if the problem of Uri Geller won't go away.

18

Split Brains

Despite decades of trying, researchers have been unable to prove to their critics' satisfaction that ESP exists. Charles Tart says that there are more than five hundred controlled experiments that show ESP and PK. He is quick to add that none of them involves Uri Geller. Tart is a parapsychologist.

Robert Ornstein is not; he is a psychologist who studies the way the brain works. Ornstein points out that most psychologists simply refuse to look at any research that conflicts with their view of the world, a view that says parapsychology is impossible.

Some research does conflict with their view, but it is all in bits and pieces. As we have seen, somehow information passes from one person to another in ways that seem to skip the normal channels of communication: sight, sound, touch. The most promising research has been done with ASCs, and some of it fits with recent advances in brain research.

The human brain has two sides, or *hemispheres*. We use the left side for logical, rational thought. Most of us use it for talking, reading, writing, and working arithmetical problems. We use the right side in creative thought, for art and music, for sensing shapes, for recognizing faces, for telling us what our feet are doing. The left side handles information in order, one thing at a time. The right side handles lots of information at once, coming up with answers that often surprise us. Most of us are also cross-wired. Each side of the brain controls the muscles on the opposite side of the body.

The two hemispheres are connected by a network of fibers called the *corpus callosum*. When this network is cut in two, one side of the brain doesn't know what the other side is doing. If such a person holds a pencil in his left hand, but cannot see it, he is unable to say what is in his hand. The right side of his brain knows that the object is a pencil, but only the left side can produce the word.

When the left hemisphere is at work — talking, reading, or solving a problem — an EEG picks up alpha waves from the right hemisphere. When the right hemisphere is on the job, the left hemisphere produces alpha waves.

Alpha is one clue to the presence of ESP. Another is relaxation, which generally means that the busy left hemisphere has been turned off.

Emotion is a third clue. When people suddenly receive messages across the miles, the word is often about danger to a loved one. In some ESP experiments, a person's like or dislike for a target picture — or for the researcher himself — seems to determine whether he hits or misses.

Dreams have been a fourth clue. We generally dream in only one of the four stages of sleep. Each stage has its own pattern of brain waves. Our dreams usually begin about an hour after we fall asleep, when we are moving from a period of deep sleep to a lighter one. In other words, when our state of consciousness has shifted.

Some researchers also think that sleep and dreams are the business of the brain's right hemisphere. EEGs show that the right side works more than the left during sleep. People whose corpus callosum has been cut say they don't dream. Robert Ornstein believes, however, that their right hemisphere dreams but their talking left half doesn't know it.

Any parapsychological talent we might have is also probably a skill that belongs to the right hemisphere. ASCs usually involve the right side of the brain and, as we have seen, the best ESP research has been done with people in such states.

But the best research is failing to convince the critics that ESP or PK even exist. No matter how carefully a study is done, critics swoop down upon it and pick it to pieces. And when they can find no flaw in the experiment, they either hint or say clearly that the researcher cheated.

Why is parapsychology having such a hard time establishing itself? There are several reasons.

First, the critics are often right. ESP research often is sloppy. The experimenter fails to consider his or her own influence or nonpsychic ways that information could pass to the subject. And when the experiment itself is carefully done, the paper that reports it frequently omits vital information, allowing critics to imagine ways that information could have been passed, ways that the researcher may have carefully guarded against but forgot to say anything about.

Fraud always haunts parapsychology. People who claim to be psychics, even those who get lots of publicity, are often frauds. D. Scott Rogo, a parapsychologist who spends a lot of time chasing down such claims, says that 90 percent of the psychics cheat all the time. What is worse, some researchers have been caught cheating.

Crooked researchers also get caught in other branches of science; one was exposed at New York's Sloan-Kettering Institute a few years ago. But because the evidence for parapsychology is weak, a crooked parapsychologist hurts the whole field in a way that a crooked medical researcher does not.

Another fact that makes the critics' job simpler is that many of the researchers are either incompetent scientists or a little crazy. The incompetent ones produce the sloppy research. About the others, parapsychologist John Beloff has said, "Parapsychology has, all through its history, suffered from its fatal attraction for persons of unbalanced mind who seek in it their personal salvation." And fellow parapsychologist D. Scott Rogo adds that the study of the paranormal "attacks both the credulous and the mentally sick." He says, "There are all too many well-meaning but incompetent people constantly running around in search of the miraculous, who are deceived not only by charlatans but by their own incorrigible will to believe."

Some researchers are true believers and, even when presented with solid evidence of fraud or natural causes, continue to swear that some psychic or parapsychological effect is genuine. They keep chasing after psychic surgery or Kirlian photography or telepathic plants. As Rogo says, "People who are involved in psychical research often don't *want* to know the truth."

Parapsychology runs into more difficulty because some incidents that seem like ESP are not psychic at all. Like the married couple in Chapter 2 who believed they were telepathic, we often pick up sights or sounds or smells when our minds are busy with something else. When these tiny clues trigger common memories, or when we seem to know something we shouldn't, we are likely to claim that our knowledge is telepathic or clairvoyant.

Although we're not aware of these signals, they register in our brains. At Harvard University, psychologist Richard Davidson connected electrodes to people and watched the recordings of their brain waves. Before them was a lighted screen, and from time to time another light would flash upon it. Sometimes the light was so bright the people noticed it; at other times it was so dim they saw nothing. Later they wore headphones and listened to a constant noise. From time to time a tone sounded. Sometimes the tone was loud; at other times it was so soft the listeners could not detect it. Yet, among 70 percent of the watchers and listeners, each time the dim light flashed or the soft tone sounded their EEGs showed a sharp change, indicating that certain parts of their brains had "seen" or "heard" the signals.

A psychiatrist found that his own ESP had such a natural explanation. Again and again, Philip Seitz worried about a former patient. Sure enough, within a day or two, the expatient would call, say that he was upset, and ask to see the psychiatrist. Seitz had always been a goat, but it happened so often that he began to wonder if he were psychic.

Then he thought of an explanation. Perhaps he had just forgotten about the former patients who did not call after he worried about them. So Seitz began to keep a record. He kept it for sixteen years. He found that two-thirds of the patients he worried about *did* call. The chances were only one in a hundred of that being accidental.

Seitz was on the verge of switching from goat to sheep, but he decided to look more closely at each case, just to be sure. When he examined his notes, he discovered that seven out of every eight patients who called became upset at the time he worried about them. But the psychiatrist was not being clairvoyant. Both the patients' upsets and the psychiatrist's worries took place on the anniversary of a disturbing event in the patients' lives.

In one case, Seitz became concerned about a former patient on Labor Day. The next day, the patient called and made an appointment. The records showed that every year the patient became depressed on Labor Day, the anniversary of his sister's death. What is more, Seitz's notes showed that one year the patient had said to him, "I heard acorns falling on the roof this morning. It reminded me that fall is here, and made me feel depressed." Shortly before Seitz became concerned about this patient, a falling acorn struck the roof of his car.

When such natural events are confused with parapsychology, the difficult job of tracking down the workings of ESP and PK becomes nearly impossible.

Another factor that makes people regard parapsychology with suspicion is its conflict with our expectations of the world. Ours is a "left hemisphere" culture. It is based on logical, rational science and the written word. This means that we use our left brains most of the time.

Our schools, set up to teach reading, writing, and arithmetic, spend most of their time educating our left brains. They do such a good job that we often refuse to accept information from our right hemispheres. We know, or think we know, what the world is like. When we come across something that doesn't fit, we force it into a familiar pattern, as most people do when they refuse to see a red ace of spades.

Perhaps people with parapsychological abilities are people who can listen to their right hemispheres. One study has shown that we know more than we know. Charles Tart once hooked up college students to EEGs. When their brain waves were being recorded, he left them and went to another room, where he connected himself to a machine that gave him electric shocks. From time to time, and Tart never knew when it would happen, the machine gave him a jolt of electricity. The students had no way of knowing when the electricity would strike, but each time Tart got a shock, the students' brains reacted.

Although our orderly, predictable culture can't explain that, perhaps one day parapsychologists will.

INDEX